Raising A Virtuous Child

al-Burāq Publications

Copyright

ISBN: 978-1-956276-25-1
Printed and published by al-Burāq Publications.
Translated and annotated by al-Burāq Publications. Where needed, context and transliterations were added. Some minor edits were made to the translated Arabic text.

Ordering Information
We offer discounts and promotions for wholesale purchases, non-profit organizations, and other educational institutions. Contact us at the email below for further information.

www.al-Buraq.org
publications@al-Buraq.org

First Edition | September 2022

إنا لله وإنا إليه راجعون

'Indeed we belong to God, and to Him do we indeed return'

بسم الله الرحمن الرحيم
الحمد لله رب العالمين الرحمن الرحيم
مالك يوم الدين إياك نعبد وإياك نستعين
اهدنا الصراط المستقيم صراط الذين
أنعمت عليهم غير المغضوب عليهم
ولا الضالين

This book was published in the name of

The Late Mohamed Jamil Saleh Homayed (Hamee)

Born: 1-31-1980 | Passed: 03-13-2022

Beloved Father of:
Fatimeh Homayed
Mariam Homayed
Zeinab Homayed

Kindly recite

Sūrat al-Fātiḥah upon his soul

We begin by giving all praise and thanks to God ﷻ for giving us the tawfiq to translate this book. He has guided us and without Him, we would not have been guided to the straight path embodied by the Prophet Muḥammad ﷺ and the Ahl al-Bayt ﻋ.

This book is dedicated to all the scholars, martyrs and believers who worked tirelessly to promote the pure Muḥammadan path.

We want to also give our thanks and appreciation to all believers from around the world and acknowledge the team which helped al-Burāq Publications complete this work, spending countless hours to make its publication possible. Please recite Sūrat al-Fātiḥah on behalf of them, their families, and their marḥūmīn.

Duʿāʾ al-Ḥujjah

اللَّهُمَّ كُنْ لِوَلِيِّكَ الْحُجَّةِ ابْنِ الْحَسَنِ صَلَوَاتُكَ
عَلَيْهِ وَعَلَى آبَائِهِ فِي هَذِهِ السَّاعَةِ وَفِي كُلِّ
سَاعَةٍ وَلِيًّا وَحَافِظًا وَقَائِدًا وَنَاصِرًا وَدَلِيلًا
وَعَيْنًا حَتَّى تُسْكِنَهُ أَرْضَكَ طَوْعًا وَتُمَتِّعَهُ فِيهَا طَوِيلًا

O God, be, for Your representative, the Ḥujjat (proof), son of al-Ḥasan, Your blessings be upon him and his forefathers, in this hour and in every hour: a guardian, a protector, a leader, a helper, a proof, and an eye - until You make him live on the Earth, in obedience (to You), and cause him to live in it for a long time.

Terms of Respect

The following Arabic phrases have been used throughout this book in their respective places to show the reverence which the noble personalities deserve.

عَزَّ وَجَلَّ

Used for God, meaning:
Exalted and Sublime (Perfect) is He

ﷺ

Used for Prophet Muḥammad, meaning:
Blessings from God be upon him and his family

عليه السلام

Used for a man (singular) of a high status, meaning:
Peace be upon him

عليها السلام

Used for a woman (singular) of a high status, meaning:
Peace be upon her

عليهما السلام

Used for men/women (dual) of a high status, meaning:
Peace be upon them both

عليهم السلام

Used for men and/or women (plural) of a high status, meaning:
Peace be upon them all

عجّل الله فرجه الشريف

Used for Imām Muḥammad al-Mahdī, meaning:
May God hasten his return

قدّس سرّه

Used for a deceased scholar, meaning:
May his resting [burial] place remain pure

Transliteration Table

The method of transliteration of Islamic terminology from the Arabic language has been carried out according to the standard transliteration table below.

ء	ʾ	ر	r	ف	f
ا	a	ز	z	ق	q
ب	b	س	s	ك	k
ت	t	ش	sh	ل	l
ث	th	ص	ṣ	م	m
ج	j	ض	ḍ	ن	n
ح	ḥ	ط	ṭ	و	w
خ	kh	ظ	ẓ	هـ	h
د	d	ع	ʿ	ي	y
ذ	dh	غ	gh		
Long Vowels					
ا	ā	و	ū	ي	ī
Short Vowels					
ــَـ	a	ــُـ	u	ــِـ	i

Table of Contents

Preamble

بسم الله الرحمن الرحيم

In the Name of God, the Beneficent, the Merciful

May God's peace and benediction be upon the master of mankind, Muḥammad and his immaculate progeny.

The late devout scholar, Āyatullāh Sayyid Khumaynī, said,"... This is Islam; it seeks to raise man into a human being. It arranges this matter even before the married couple is espoused; as it determines the obligations of the man and woman who intend on getting married. Then it states the behavioral conditions that must be observed by them until the child is conceived, what they must do during the nursing period and how they must behave with the child while he is in his parents' custody. Then it determines how they must deal with him in the environment of the early, middle, and high school[years]; in addition to the quality of the educators who handle the upbringing of children. And when the child reaches the age of puberty, Islam sets out for him the modality according to which his actions, ethics and behavior should be, in addition to that which he must avoid. All this is due to the fact that Islam wants to support the community by raising virtuous individuals."[1]

---

[1] *Makanat Al-Mar'a fi Fikr Āyatullāh Sayyid Khumaynī*, publications of the embassy of the Islamic Republic, Damascus, p. 141-147.

Despite the huge efforts made with the Islamic provisions in pursuit of raising a virtuous child, as observed by the readers of the Noble Qur'ān and the ḥadīth of the Prophet ﷺ and his progeny ﵈, we find that the community remains distant from these provisions in many of its details.

Therefrom arose the idea of delivering this small book in order to encourage people to read it.

May God accept these humble efforts and render them ammunition of ours on the day of Resurrection.

The Value and Impact of a Virtuous Child

"A virtuous child is one of Heaven's (basil) flowers."[2]

Through this amazing articulation, the Prophet of Islam ﷺ shows the great blessing bestowed by God on man when He grants him a virtuous child. For, he is like a (basil) flower that fills its surroundings with a fragrance which comforts the spirit and fills the heart with joy and delight. Nonetheless, he is not one the worldly life's (basil) flowers, rather one of the Heaven's. For, the (basil) flower of the worldly life hasn't reached the position with which a virtuous child can be

---

[2] al-Ḥurr al-ʿĀmilī, Shaykh Muḥammad b. al-Ḥasan, *Wasā'il al-Shī'a*, verified by al-Shirazi, published by Dar 'Ih'ya' al-Turath al-'Arabi, Beirut, Vol. 15, p. 97.

compared. That's why the Prophet ﷺ compared him to the Heaven's (basil) flowers; and Imām Jaʿfar al-Ṣādiq ؑ emphasized on his noble Grandfather's ḥadīth when he said – in a narration on his behalf, "One of man's joys is a virtuous child."[3]

The Impact of a Virtuous Child in the Worldly Life

His impact in this worldly life is not concealed from anyone, whether from the community that benefits from him or his parents who resort to him.

This is narrated by Imām Zayn al-ʿĀbidīn ؑ : "One of man's joys is to have a child to whom he can resort to for support."[4]

The Impact of a Virtuous Child in the Intermediate World (The World of Barzakh)

The impact of the child extends, after the death of his parents, in such a way that his good deeds escort his parents, lighten up their grave with a divine light and protect them from the dreadful horror of the grave. In fact, it might even change the parent's fate from suffering to bliss.

---

[3] Ibid.

[4] Ibid., p. 356, ḥadīth (27286/7)

The Prophet ﷺ points out this truth in the following ḥadīth mentioned by him:

"There are five categories of people whose reward follows them to their graves:

1. He who sows a palm tree.
2. He who digs up a well.
3. He who builds a mosque.
4. He who writes a copy of the Noble Qur'ān.
5. He who leaves behind a virtuous child."[5]

Imām Ja'far al-Ṣādiq ؑ emphasized on this subject when he ؑ said, "When a man dies, he ceases to benefit from any reward save from the following three:

1. An alms which had been carried out during his life; for, it continues after his death.
2. A practice of guidance which he had established; for, it is implemented after his death.

[5] Majlisī, 'Allamah Muḥammad Bāqir, *Biḥār al-Anwār*, published by al-Wafa' institute, Beirut, 3rd edition, 1403, Vol. 104, p. 100.

3. A virtuous child who pleads forgiveness on his behalf."[6]

Also, as a practical implementation of this truth, the Great Prophet ﷺ narrates a story that happened to the Prophet of God, 'Īsā ؑ. He ﷺ said, "'Īsā bin Maryam passed by a grave whose owner was suffering; then he passed by it again at a later time to find that the owner was not suffering anymore. So he said, O Lord, I passed by this grave one year to find his owner in torment, then I passed by it this year to find that he was not suffering. So, God revealed to him, O Spirit of God, he had conceived of a virtuous child who fixed a road and sheltered an orphan, so I forgave him for what his son had done."[7]

One of the interesting things that have been told in this regard is that someone said, "I was ascetic in having children until I stood in 'Arafa, and next to me was a young boy crying and supplicating to God saying, O Lord, my parents, my parents; thus, I felt the desire of having children after hearing that."[8]

---

[6] Ibid., p. 100.

[7] Ibid., p. 101.

[8] Al-Ḥurr al-'Āmilī, Shaykh Muḥammad b. al-Ḥasan, *Wasā'il al-Shī'a*, Vol. 15, p. 95.

The Impact of a Virtuous Child on Survival from the Hellfire

The good impact of a virtuous child extends to the Hereafter, such that his virtuousness rescues the parents from the Hellfire which they have earned through their deeds. Nonetheless, they left behind them a daughter who wore the modest clothing of Islam (*ḥijāb*) and maintained her chastity through it. Thus, her hijab becomes a veil that stands between her parents and the Hellfire. This was narrated to us on behalf of the Honest & the Trustworthy ﷺ, that He ﷺ said, "The best of children are the veiled girls; he who has one, God renders her a veil that protects him from the Hellfire."[9]

A Virtuous Child is the Supplication of the Prophets (a)

Due to the value and great benefits of a virtuous child, the grant of a virtuous child was the supplication of the great prophets of God.

The Noble Qur'ān spoke to us of the supplication of the Prophet of God, Zakariyyā (a) by saying:

---

[9] Majlisī, ʿAllamah Muḥammad Bāqir, *Biḥār al-Anwār*, Vol. 104, p. 91.

﴿هُنالِكَ دَعا زَكَرِيّا رَبَّهُ ۖ قالَ رَبِّ هَب لي مِن لَدُنكَ ذُرِّيَّةً طَيِّبَةً ۖ إِنَّكَ سَميعُ الدُّعاءِ﴾

﴾hunālika da'ā zakariyyā rabbahū qāla rabbi hab lī min ladunka dhurriyyatan ṭayyibatan 'innaka samī'u d-du'ā﴿

﴾Thereat Zechariah supplicated his Lord. He said, 'My Lord! Grant me a good offspring from You! Indeed You hear all supplications.'﴿[10]

Therefore, we ought to exert massive efforts in building a virtuous child while supplicating – first and foremost - to God ﷻ, asking Him ﷻ to fulfill this great gift and benefiting from the Islamic teachings which focused on the influential factors for producing virtuous children, starting from setting the intention towards marriage, passing through multiple stations including choosing a spouse and copulating with her, her nutrition during her pregnancy, the actions done with the child at the moment of birth and afterwards until he becomes eligible for upbringing in accordance with the will of God and by resorting to the approaches defined accurately by the sacred *Sharī'a*.

Accordingly, let's take a look at the Islamic beams which – through its glowing light – illuminates the road that leads to making a virtuous child.

---

[10] Sūrat Āl 'Imrān, Verse 38.

"All the existing sects in the world have limited their interests to the mature human being who has reached the stage of understanding and perception... whereas, Islam stipulates provisions for man even before his birth; for, it determines for the parents – before their marriage – the nature of the person to be chosen by each of them. It tells the girl which man to choose, and sets for the man the qualifications of the desired wife."

Why does Islam do that?

"Because each, the man and woman, will become sources from which other individuals are created. Islam wants the individual, who will join society later on, to be virtuous."[11]

[11] *Al-Mar'a fi Fikr Āyatullāh Sayyid Khumaynī*, p. 146.

The Reasons for Virtuousness Outside the Realm of Upbringing

Before Birth

The Prophet of Islam and the immaculate Imāms pointed out to the factors that influence the creation of a virtuous child before his birth. We will present these factors below.

Supplication Before Marriage

Islam started the project of preparing for a virtuous child by guiding the man, who sets his intention to get married, towards supplicating to God and asking Him for a virtuous child. It is narrated that Imām Jaʿfar al-Ṣādiq said, "If he proceeds with this, let him pray two units of prayer, give praise to God and say, "O God, I want to get married. O God, decree for me the chastest of women, most protective of me in herself and in my money, most extensive in sustenance and the most blessed. And decree for me, from her, a virtuous child and make him my successor in my life and after my death."[12]

---

[12] Al-Ḥurr al-ʿĀmilī, Shaykh Muḥammad b. al-Ḥasan, *Wasāʾil al-Shīʿa*, Vol. 14, p. 79.

Choosing the Husband and Wife

Islam proceeded with its guidance towards that which influences the creation of a virtuous child, as we observe in the aḥadīth of the Infallibles ﷺ. For, it is narrated that Amīr al-Mu'minīn, Imām 'Alī b. Abī Ṭālib ؑ said, "Don't ever marry an idiotic woman; for, her company is a tribulation and her child is lost."[13]

This ḥadīth, amongst others, aligns with what has been proven in regards to the role of genetics in establishing a person's personality, which was pointed out in the famous ḥadīth "Roots [inherited genes] are intrusive", as confirmed by modern science.

The scholar Mandel says, "Many of the genetic attributes are transferred without division or alteration from one or both parents to the descendant."[14]

Amīr al-Mu'minīn, Imām 'Alī b. Abī Ṭālib ؑ confirmed the impact of genetics on the child in two stances:

Firstly, when he asked his son Muḥammad b. al-Hanafiyya, on the day of the battle of al-Jamal to attack the opposing army, Muḥammad paused a little bit.

---

[13] Bayḍūn, Labīb, *Tasnīf Nahj al-Balāgha*, publications of the office of Islamic press, Qom, 2nd edition, 1408 AH, p. 793.

[14] al-Qarashī, Bāqir Sharīf, *Hayāt al-Imām al-Ḥusayn* ؑ, publications of Dār al-Kutub al-'Ilmiyya, Qom, Vol. 1, p. 43.

Then the Imām ʿ repeated his command by saying, "Attack", so he answered him, "O Amīr al-Muʾminīn, don't you see that the arrows are falling like heavy, massive rain?" Then the Imām ʿ pushed him in his chest and told him, "You have been affected by your mother's genes."[15]

Secondly, when he wanted to have strong and brave sons who would support his son al-Ḥusayn ʿ in Karbalāʾ; so he told his brother ʿAqīl who was knowledgeable in the news and ancestries of the Arabs, "Bring me a woman who was conceived by the bravest of the Arabs, so I can marry her so that she conceives for me a brave young knight." So he said to him, "What do you think of Fāṭima, the daughter of Huzam bin Khalid al-Kilabiyya? There isn't amongst the Arabs anyone who is braver than her ancestors, nor more knightly. Thus, Amīr al-Muʾminīn, Imām ʿAlī b. Abī Ṭālib ʿ married her and she conceived for him several children, the first of whom was al-Abbās.[16]

Copulating with the Wife

Islam provided guidance towards several issues that influence the creation of a virtuous child during

---

[15] al-Amīn, Muḥsin, *Aʿyān al-Shīʿa*, publications of Dār al-Taʿaruf, Beirut, p. 457.

[16] Ibid., Vol. 7, p. 429.

copulation with one's wife; so he directed towards the following:

a. Naming and Supplication before Copulation

It was mentioned on behalf of Abdul Raḥmān bin Kathīr: I was sitting with Abī Abdillah's when he mentioned the devil's share and magnified it until he scared me. So I said, "May I be sacrificed for you, how can one escape that? So he said, "If you wanted to have intercourse say: In the name of God, the most Gracious, the most Merciful, O God if you decree for me a successor on this night, don't allow the devil to have a share or portion or opportunity in him; and make him a believer who is pure and refined from the devil and his evil, majestic is Your praise."[17]

It is narrated that Amīr al-Mu'minīn, Imām ʿAlī b. Abī Ṭālib said, "If any of you copulated (with his wife), then he should say: In the name of God, and by God, O God avert me from the devil, and avert the devil from the sustenance which you have provided me." He said, "Thus, if God decreed a child for them, the devil will not harm him in any way at all."[18]

---

[17] Al-Ḥurr al-ʿĀmilī, Shaykh Muḥammad b. al-Ḥasan, *Wasāʾil al-Shīʿa*, Vol. 14, p. 97.

[18] Ibid., p. 96.

b. Choosing the Appropriate Timings (for copulation)

The narrations mentioned several timings during which copulation, therein, influences the future of the child. Of these timings is what was mentioned by Imām Abu Ja'far ﷺ once he was asked whether there's a timing during which copulation is detested. He ﷺ, thus, answered, "Yes,

From the rise of dawn until sunrise,

And from sunset until the disappearance of the twilight,

And on the night of a lunar eclipse,

And on the night of a solar eclipse,

And during the day and night of an earthquake,

And during the yellow or black or red wind...

By Him who sent Muḥammad ﷺ with the Prophecy, and specialized him with the message, and chose him with grace, none of you shall copulate during any of those timings and conceive a child which provides him with peacefulness."[19]

Nutrition during Pregnancy

Islam drew attention towards the role of nutrition in the child's future and beauty. It started with the nutrition which establishes a man's sperm and its impact on the child. Thus, it praised certain types of foods such as pomegranate and quince; for, it was mentioned that Imām Ja'far al-Ṣādiq said, "He who eats quince on an empty stomach will have good sperm and a beautiful child."[20] Moreover, it was mentioned that al-Khurasani said, "Eating pomegranate increases a man's sperm and beautifies one's child."[21]

Narrations emphasized on the impact of a pregnant woman's nutrition on the future of her pregnancy. We will present, below, some of what was mentioned in this regard.

---

[19] Al-Mīrzā al-Nūrī, *Mustadrak al-Wasā'il*, verified and published by the institute of Ahl al-Bayt li-'Ihya' al-Turath, Qom, 1st edition, 1407 AH, Vol. 14, p. 223-224.

[20] Majlisī, 'Allamah Muḥammad Bāqir, *Biḥār al-Anwār*, Vol. 104, p. 81.

[21] Ibid., p. 83.

Drinking Frankincense

It is narrated that the Prophet ﷺ said, "Quench your pregnant women with frankincense, for it increases the boy's intellect."[22]

Eating Quince

It is narrated that the Prophet ﷺ said, "Feed your pregnant women with quince; for, it enhances your children's morality."[23]

Eating Watermelon

It is narrated that the Prophet ﷺ said, "There isn't any pregnant woman who eats watermelon except that her child has a beautiful face and temperament."[24]

These are a few prenatal influential factors. Behold that which influences the virtuousness of the child during the first days after birth.

"When you look at Islam, you find out that it possesses a holistic humane system. It even has regulations for the

---

[22] Al-Mīrzā al-Nūrī, *Mustadrak al-Wasā'il*, Vol. 15, p. 137.

[23] Ibid., Vol. 15, p. 135.

[24] Ibid., Vol. 15, p. 214, ḥadīth (18038/14).

period preceding a person's birth and preceding his parents' marriage, so that the seed is sowed in a wholesome land. For, Islam gives its opinion in regards to the selection of the husband and wife, the appropriate circumstances for marriage and its etiquettes, the etiquettes of the bed and the pregnancy period, as would a farmer who lays a seed and is keen on taking care of it and constantly nurturing it until it grows in proper manner."[25]

The First Days after Birth

Islam continued in mentioning the influential factors of building a virtuous child from the moment of birth. So, it provided the following directions.

'Adhān and Iqāmah at the Moment of Birth

Islam took care that the first word the newborn hears is the word "God", by emphasizing on the desirability of reading the 'Adhān in the newborn's right years and the Iqāmah in his left ear, due to the influence of this reading on the virtuousness of the child in his future. For, it is narrated that the Messenger of God ﷺ said, "He who has a newborn should read the 'Adhān of

[25] *Al-Mar'a fi Fikr Āyatullāh Sayyid Khumaynī,* p. 146.

prayer in his right ear and the Iqāmah in his left ear. For, it is a protection from the accursed devil."[26]

Moreover, it was mentioned by Asma' that after the birth of al-Ḥusayn, the Prophet came and told her, "O Asma', behold my son, so she put him in a white piece of cloth, then he read the 'Adhān in his right ear and the Iqāmah in his left."[27]

Breastfeeding

Islam gave great importance to the nursing period, as it clarified this significance on the nursing child's future.

The Mother Takes Precedence in Breastfeeding

The Infallibles clarified that the newborn's mother takes precedence over all other women in nursing him, and that the finest breast milk is that of his mother's. Modern science has emphasized this point, as well. For, it is narrated that the Prophet of Islam said, "The boy has no finer milk than his mother's."[28]

---

26 Al-Ḥurr al-'Āmilī, Shaykh Muḥammad b. al-Ḥasan, *Wasā'il al-Shī'a*, Vol. 15, p. 136.

27 Majlisī, 'Allamah Muḥammad Bāqir, *Biḥār al-Anwār*, Vol. 104, p. 111.

28 Al-Ḥurr al-'Āmilī, Shaykh Muḥammad b. al-Ḥasan, *Wasā'il al-Shī'a*, Vol. 15, p. 188.

It is also narrated that Amīr al-Mu'minīn, Imām 'Alī b. Abī Ṭālib said, "There isn't any milk fed to the boy more blessed for him than his mother's."[29]

In pursuit of encouraging the mother to breastfeed her child, the Prophet clarified the reward of nursing by saying, "If a woman gets pregnant, she takes the position of the one who fasts all day and worships in the night and the one who struggles through himself and his money for the sake of God. When she gives birth, she is granted a reward which is unknown to anyone due to its greatness. When she breastfeeds, she is granted – with every suck – the reward of freeing a slave of the children of Ismael. Then when she is done breastfeeding, a noble angel pats her on her side and says proceed, for you have been forgiven."[30]

The Impact of Being Breastfed by Someone besides the Mother

The narrations of the Infallibles warned of the inaccuracy in selecting a nursing woman for the newborn other than his/her mother, while pointing out to the impact of the nursing woman's milk on the morality and temperament of the nursing child. For, it is narrated that Amīr al-Mu'minīn, Imām 'Alī b. Abī

---

[29] Ibid., p. 175.

[30] Ibid., p. 175.

Ṭālib said, "Watch out for the person who breastfeeds your children; for, the child grows on it (the milk)."[31]

It is also narrated by him, "Be selective of those who nurse your children as you are selective in regards to your spouses; for, breastfeeding changes one's temperament."[32]

Do Not Have Those Breastfeed Your Children

Therefore, the Infallibles prohibited having the women who possess the following qualifications as nursing women.

1. The Idiot

It is narrated that Amīr al-Mu'minīn, Imām 'Alī b. Abī Ṭālib said, "Do not have an idiot breastfeed your child; for, the milk dominates the temperament."[33]

2. The Woman with Blurred Eyesight

It is narrated that the Prophet said, "Do not have the idiot or the woman with a blurred eyesight breastfeed

---

[31] Ibid., p. 188.

[32] Ibid., p. 188.

[33] Ibid., Vol. 15, p. 188.

your child; for, milk is contagious."[34] The woman with blurred eyesight is a woman who suffers from a disease in her eyes, which is the flow of tears in such a way that almost prevents her from seeing through them.[35]

3. The Ugly Woman

For, it is narrated that Imām Abī Ja'far said, "... Do not have an ugly woman breastfeed your child; for, milk might be contagious."[36]

4. A Nasibi Woman

And she is a woman who carries, within her heart, animosity against the Ahl al-Bayt . For, it is narrated that Imām Ja'far al-Ṣādiq said, "The breastfeeding of a Jewish or Christian woman is better than that of a Nasibi."[37]

---

[34] Ibid.

[35] B. Manzour, *Lisan al-'Arab*, publications of Dār al-Fikr, Beirut, Vol. 6, p. 327.

[36] Al-Ḥurr al-'Āmilī, Shaykh Muḥammad b. al-Ḥasan, *Wasā'il al-Shī'a*, Vol. 15, p. 189.

[37] Ibid., p. 187.

5. A Fornicator or a Daughter of a Fornicator

Imām Mūsā al-Kāẓim was asked, "Is it appropriate to have a fornicator breastfeed one's child?" He answered, "No, nor her daughter who was conceived from fornication."[38]

6. The Insane Woman

It is narrated that the Prophet said, "Beware of having your children breastfeed from a prostitute or an insane woman; for, milk is contagious."[39]

Have the Following Women Breastfeed your Children

On the other hand, Ahl al-Bayt encouraged the requirement of having the nursing woman – after the mother – possess good qualifications in terms of physical features and morality.

For, it is narrated that Imām Abi Ja'far said, "Let your child breastfeed from beautiful women."[40]

---

[38] Ibid.

[39] Majlisī, 'Allamah Muḥammad Bāqir, *Biḥār al-Anwār*, Vol. 104, p. 96.

[40] Al-Ḥurr al-'Āmilī, Shaykh Muḥammad b. al-Ḥasan, *Wasā'il al-Shī'a*, Vol. 15, p. 189.

And in another narration, "You should have the clean and beautiful woman breastfeed your children; for, milk is contagious."[41]

The Impact of Pure Milk

One of the delightful stories narrated in regards to the impact of pure milk is that of the two noblemen al-Murtaḍā and al-Raḍī when they split their father's inheritance after his death leaving one last book for both of them. Al-Sharīf al-Raḍī (the one who collected Nahj al-Balāgha) told his brother, as he tried to have the book for himself, "This book belongs to the one who hasn't committed an unlawful act in his life", and he wanted to take the book. Then, his brother – Sayyid al-Murtaḍā - surprised him – and he was a Shīʿa jurisprudential Marjiʿ in his time – when he told him, "This book belongs to the one who has never thought of committing an unlawful act in his life, thus, I will be taking it."

When we go back to the history of these two great men to study the factors of their upbringing, we realize that their mother used to perform ablution every time she breastfed them, which confirms the impact of pure nutrition and spiritual etiquettes on the future of the children.

---

[41] Those who are clean and beautiful.

The poet was truthful when he said,

"May God refrain from harming my mother; for she drank from the love of the *wali* (Guardian) and fed it to me through her milk.

And I had a father who was in love with Abā al-Ḥasan; thus, from here and there, I became fond of Abī al-Ḥasan."

Massage the roof of the baby's mouth (*Taḥnīk*)

One of the things that has an impact on the virtuousness of the child and is considered a desirable act in Islam is massaging the roof of the baby's mouth with something. Taḥnīk means inserting something in the mouth and massaging it into the palate.[42]

---

[42] Al-Tarihi, Fakhr al-Dīn, *Majma' al-Bahrain wa Matla' al-Nairain*, verified by al-Husseini, publications of the al-Wafa' Institute, Beirut, 2nd edition, 1403 AH, Vol. 5, p. 263.

As for the desirable material for *taḥnīk*, it's the following:

1. Ḥusaynī Soil (*turba*)

It is narrated that Imām Jaʿfar al-Ṣādiq said, "perform *taḥnīk* with the soil of al-Ḥusayn; for, it provides security."[43]

2. The Water of the Euphrates

It is narrated that Imām Jaʿfar al-Ṣādiq said, "I don't suppose any (child) is given water from the Euphrates for *taḥnīk*, except that he loves us Ahl al-Bayt."[44]

3. Honey

In the book 'The Jurisprudence of al-Riḍā, it is mentioned: "perform *taḥnīk on your newborn using* water from the Euphrates if you manage to provide it, or with honey once he is born."[45]

---

[43] Al-Mīrzā al-Nūrī, *Mustadrak al-Wasāʾil*, Vol. 15, p. 138.

[44] Ibid., p. 139.

[45] Ibid., p. 138.

4. Dates

It is narrated that Amīr al-Mu'minīn, Imām 'Alī b. Abī Ṭālib said, "perform *taḥnīk* on your children with dates; for this is what the Messenger of God did with al-Ḥasan and al-Ḥusayn."[46]

Having the Mother Eat Dates during her Postpartum Period

It is narrated that the Prophet said, "Let the first thing a woman eats after giving birth be dates; for, God had told Maryam: {Shake the trunk of the palm tree, freshly picked dates will drop upon you.} It was said: O Messenger of God, what if it wasn't a season for dates; he said: "seven dates from those of Medina, if not then seven dates from your own countries; for, God says: "By My Glory and Majesty, and Greatness and High Stance, there isn't any woman who eats fresh ripe dates on the day she gives birth except that her child becomes patient."[47]

"Islam took interest in man's life stages starting from the moment he is born, passing through the period of pregnancy, breastfeeding, upbringing in his mother's

[46] Al-Ḥurr al-'Āmilī, Shaykh Muḥammad b. al-Ḥasan, *Wasā'il al-Shī'a*, Vol. 15, p. 138.

[47] Ibid., Vol. 15, p. 134.

arms and puberty, all the way until death, the grave and life after the grave.

There isn't any human law that has taken these matters under its custody; for, these matters are taken care of by the laws of the Prophets."[48]

It is desirable to perform Ghusl to the newborn once he is born while taking care of protecting him from any harm, to read the 'Adhān in his right ear and the Iqāmah in his left, and perform *taḥnīk* using the water from the Euphrates and the soil of the Master of Martyrs ﷷ.[49]

It is desirable for the newborn to breastfeed from his mother; for, it is more blessed than others, unless there were circumstances that demanded another woman due to her honor and good character and malignancy of the mother.

The breastfeeding period is deemed complete at two full years (twenty four months); and it is acceptable to complete it three months earlier at twenty one months. And it is not acceptable to reduce it less than that where it is possible and unnecessary.[50]

---

[48] *Al-Mar'a fi Fikr Āyatullāh Sayyid Khumaynī*, p. 147.

[49] Khumaynī, Sayyid Rūhullāh Mūsawī, *Taḥrīr al-Wasīlah*, Vol. 2, p. 281.

[50] Ibid., p. 283.

Naming the Child

Parents name their children based on so many premises.

In the past, Arabs used to name their children 'leopard', 'tiger' and 'dog' because they were people of war. Thus, they wanted to intimidate their enemies through the names of their children.[51]

We notice, today, that many names are based on the admiration held for those who possess these names. For, one may admire a ruler or a great scholar or a famous celebrity or a well-known artist, and therefore, name his child after him/her.

And all this may take place while being oblivious of the negative impact of this name.

For, naming a child after an artist may play a role in making that artist a role model for the child in his life, in a way that allows the child to get influenced by him when he grows up. And naming him after an oppressive ruler may affect the child's perception of oppression.

---

[51] Ḥadīth of Imām ʿAlī al-Riḍā mentioned in this context in al-Ḥurr al-ʿĀmilī, Shaykh Muḥammad b. al-Ḥasan, *Wasa'il al-Shīʿa*, Vol. 15, p. 123 and the following pages.

Parents may grant their children foreign – rather than Arabic – names due to being attracted to the pronunciation of the foreign language while being oblivious to its impact on the child in terms of his attachment to those communities and love of detaching from the Islamic community.

Moreover, parents may choose some names that carry bad content such as 'oppressive' or 'seduction' and their likes without noticing their negative influence.

Islam's Interest in Names

Islam came and invited people to select beautiful names for their children considering it one of the child's primary rights upon the parents. For, it is mentioned that a man came to the Prophet ﷺ and asked him, "What is the right of my son? He ﷺ answered, "That you give him a good name, teach him good morals and place him in a good environment."[52]

Islam established a link between the name of one's child and the calling on the Day of Resurrection, when the Prophet ﷺ said – as was mentioned on his behalf, "Select good names for your children; for, you will be called by them on the Day of Resurrection, rise O

[52] Al-Ḥurr al-'Āmilī, Shaykh Muḥammad b. al-Ḥasan, *Wasā'il al-Shī'a*, Vol. 15, p.124.

person 'x' son of person 'y' to your light, and rise O person 'a' son of person 'b' you have no light."[53]

Changing the Name

The Prophet didn't stop at this invitation; he rather practically changed the ugly names of people and even of countries as well.[54]

The Imāms of Ahl al-Bayt followed the example of the Messenger of God in the invitation and practice of changing ugly names to beautiful ones. For, one of the companions of Imām Jaʿfar al-Ṣādiq narrated that he entered to find him standing next to his son's head in the cradle, Mūsā . So, the man approached the Imām; that's when the Imām told him, "Go and change the name of your daughter whom you named yesterday; for, it is a name that is detested by God." And the man, as he spoke of himself, had named his daughter "Humeira'"; thus, the man changed her name.[55]

---

53 Ibid., p. 123.

54 al-Ḥimyarī, ʿAbd Allāh b. Jaʿfar, *Qurb al-Isnād*, verified and published by the institute of Ahl al-Bayt li ʿIhya' al-Turath, Qom, 1st edition, 1413 AH, p. 92.

55 Al-Ḥurr al-ʿĀmilī, Shaykh Muḥammad b. al-Ḥasan, *Wasāʾil al-Shīʿa*, Vol. 15, p. 123.

A Name is a Meaning and an Example

Islam invited (people) towards naming children while observing two matters:

First: The Content and Meaning

Islam called for choosing names that have the meaning of servanthood such as Abdullah (the servant of God).

It is narrated that the Prophet ﷺ said, "The best of names are Abdullah (the servant of God) and Abul Raḥmān (the servant of the most Gracious). And the worst of names are Darar, Murra, Harb and Zalem."[56]

It is also narrated that he ﷺ said, "... The most honest of names is that which means servanthood."[57]

Second: The Virtuousness of the Owner of that Name

It is narrated that the Prophet ﷺ said, as he was talking about the best of names, "The best of names are the names of prophets."[58]

---

[56] Ibid., p. 131.

[57] Majlisī, 'Allamah Muḥammad Bāqir, *Biḥār al-Anwār*, Vol. 104, p. 126.

[58] Ibid.

The Prophet of Islam ﷺ clarified the impact of naming the child after the prophets when he ﷺ said – as was narrated on his behalf, "If some of the household members were named after a prophet then the blessing of God will not leave them."[59]

It is also narrated that he ﷺ said, "There isn't any household that holds the name of a prophet except that God sends them an angel to bless them day and night."[60]

The Name Muḥammad ﷺ

Since the last of the Prophets, Muḥammad ﷺ, is the master of mankind and the best example thereof, there had been definite encouragement to name (one's child) after his honorable name. It was rather mentioned that the Prophet ﷺ had said, "He who has three boys and doesn't name either one of them Muḥammad has deserted me."[61]

Imām ʿAlī al-Riḍā ﷺ has spoken to us about the impact of naming (one's child) after the name of the noble

---

[59] Al-Mīrzā al-Nūrī, *Mustadrak al-Wasāʾil*, Vol. 15, p. 129.

[60] Majlisī, ʿAllamah Muḥammad Bāqir, *Biḥār al-Anwār*, Vol. 103, p. 129.

[61] Ibid.

Prophet ﷺ by saying, "The house which carries the name Muḥammad, its members wake up and sleep in good condition."[62]

And as an emphasis on the desirability of naming (one's child) after the name of the last Prophet ﷺ, a desirable act was mentioned in regards to naming every male in the name of Muḥammad during the first seven days after his birth, then afterwards, one may either leave the name as is or change it to another name.

It is narrated that Imām Jaʿfar al-Ṣādiq ؏ said, "We do not have any new born son except that we call him Muḥammad. Then when seven days pass, if we so desire, we change it or leave it as is."[63]

As a sign of respect to the Prophet Muḥammad ﷺ, a special treatment has been mentioned in regards to everyone who has been named after him. For, it is narrated that the Prophet ﷺ said, "If you name (your son) Muḥammad, do not abhor him, deny him or strike him. Blessed is the house who holds a Muḥammad, and a gathering which includes a Muḥammad and a companionship with a Muḥammad."[64]

---

[62] Ibid.

[63] Ibid., Vol. 104, p. 131.

[64] Majlisī, ʿAllamah Muḥammad Bāqir, *Biḥār al-Anwār*, Vol. 16, p. 239-240, and the meaning of deny here is to deny him his need.

The Names of Ahl al-Bayt

As Islam was in favor of naming (one's child) after the Prophet's name Muḥammad ﷺ due to its good impact and reinforcement of virtuous leadership, it also encouraged the naming (of one's child) after the names of the noble Ahl al-Bayt for the same reason. For, it was mentioned that someone asked the Imām: Does this benefit us? Thus, the Imām answered him, "Yes, by God, for, is religion anything but love?!!"[65]

God said:

﴿قُل إن كُنتُم تُحِبّونَ اللهَ فَاتَّبِعوني
يُحبِبكُمُ اللهُ وَيَغفِر لَكُم ذُنوبَكُم ۗ وَاللهُ غَفورٌ رَحيمٌ﴾

﴿qul 'in kuntum tuḥibbūna llāha fa-ttabi'ūnī yuḥbibkumu llāhu wa-yaghfir lakum dhunūbakum wa-llāhu ghafūrun raḥīmun﴾

﴾Say, 'If you love God, then follow me; God will love you and forgive you your sins, and God is all-forgiving, all-merciful'﴿[66]

---

[65] Ibid., p. 130.

[66] Sūrat Āl 'Imrān, Verse 31.

It is narrated that Imām Abi al-Ḥasan said, "Poverty does not enter a house that holds a member whose name is Muḥammad or Ahmad or Alī or al-Ḥasan or al-Ḥusayn or Ja'far or Talib or Abdullah or Fāṭima from the women."[67]

The Name 'Alī

And of the names of Ahl al-Bayt, the infallible Ahl al-Bayt emphasized on naming (one's child) with the name 'Alī. Hadīth have shown the good impact of this blessed name; for, it was mentioned that Imām al-Bāqir said to B. Saghīr, "What is your name?" He replied, "Muḥammad." The Imam asked, "What is your nickname?" He replied,: "'Alī."Abu Ja'far said, "You have strictly protected yourself from the devil. When the devil hears someone call: O; Muḥammad or O Ali, he melts away like lead."[68]

The name 'Alī has a story in the history of the Umayyads who declared a war against this blessed name. For, as narrated by B. Hijr, "if they heard of a newborn named 'Alī they would kill him."[69]

---

[67] Al-Ḥurr al-'Āmilī, Shaykh Muḥammad b. al-Ḥasan, *Wasā'il al-Shī'a*, Vol. 15, p. 128-129.

[68] Ibid., p. 126.

[69] Askarī, Sayyid Murtaḍa Sharīf, *Ma'ālim al-Madrasatayn*, publications of al-Ba'tha institute, Qom, Vol. 1, p. 385.

Moreover, people used to get close to the rulers by abhorring the name ʿAlī. Once, someone approached al-Hajjaj and said to him, "O prince, my parents have dishonored me by naming me ʿAlī; and I am poor, miserable and in need of connecting to the prince." Thus, al-Hajjaj entertained him with laughter and said, "Your imploration was delightful; and I have granted you the following."[70]

Thus, during the Umayyad mandate, the name ʿAlī represented a horror which rendered people terrified of mentioning it. Even when they recited narrations related to religious rulings, they would say 'Abu Zeinab' or 'the Shaykh' said, instead of 'Alī said'.[71]

That's why Imām al-Ḥusayn was in the middle of this battle over the name ʿAlī when he named all his sons by the name of ʿAlī. Thus, he had ʿAlī al-Akbar, ʿAlī al-Asghar (the nursing baby Abdullah) and ʿAlī Zayn al-ʿĀbidīn. And he used to say: "If I had a hundred sons,

---

[70] al-Amīn, Muḥsin, *Aʿyān al-Shīʿa*, publications of Dār al-Ma'arif, Beirut, Vol. 1, p. 27.

[71] Shams al-Dīn, Muḥammad Mahdī, *Thawrat al-Ḥusayn*, publications of Dār al-Ma'arif, 5th edition, Beirut, p. 69.

I wouldn't have loved to name either one of them except by 'Alī."[72]

The Name Fāṭima

Islam gave an advantage for the name 'Fāṭimah' in reverence of Sayyidah al-Zahrā' . For, it has been mentioned that poverty does not enter a house that holds a girl whose name is Fāṭimah.

It was mentioned that al-Sukūnī said: I went to Abī Abdillah while I was distressed, so he said to me: O Sukūnī, what caused you distress? I said: I have just had a newborn girl. So he said: "O Sukūnī, it is but the earth which carries her weight, and God who manages her sustenance. She lives a lifespan that isn't yours and eats from a sustenance separate from yours." Then, by God, he felt joyous on my behalf. Then he said: What did you name her? I said: Fāṭima. He said: Oh Oh Oh, then he put his hand on his forehead until he said: "If you named her Fāṭimah, then do not insult her, curse her, or hit her."[73]

---

[72] Al-Ḥurr al-ʿĀmilī, Shaykh Muḥammad b. al-Ḥasan, *Wasāʾil al-Shīʿa*, Vol. 15, p. 128.

[73] Al-Ḥurr al-ʿĀmilī, Shaykh Muḥammad b. al-Ḥasan, *Wasāʾil al-Shīʿa*, Vol. 15, p. 20.

The Boy's Nickname

In the same way Islam took care of good naming, it also took interest in good nicknames. From there arose the Noble Prophet's ﷺ invitation towards choosing good nicknames by saying: "He is to be given the best of names and the best of nicknames."[74]

However, some nicknames are detested such as the nickname Abī al-Qassem with the name Muḥammad[75]; for, this nickname with this name is specifically related to the noble Prophet ﷺ. And in pursuit of strengthening the bond between the father and his son, Islam encouraged the practice of giving the son a nickname with his father's name. So, if his father's name is Ali, the boy would be nicknamed 'Abī Alī'. Having a nickname after his father's name will increase the boy's feelings of amicability towards his father. For, it is narrated that the Prophet ﷺ said: "The Sunnah and virtuousness lie in nicknaming the man by his father's name."[76]

---

[74] Majlisī, 'Allamah Muḥammad Bāqir, *Biḥār al-Anwār*, Vol. 104, p. 126.

[75] Ibid.

[76] Majlisī, 'Allamah Muḥammad Bāqir, *Biḥār al-Anwār*, Vol. 104, p. 131.

And after the naming come certain actions that have an impact on the virtuousness of the child. These actions are determined to take place on the seventh day after the child's birth. They will be discussed below.

It is desirable to give the newborn beautiful names; for, this is of the child's rights upon his father. And the best of these names are those which carry the meaning of servanthood to God ﷻ such as Abdullah, Abul Raḥīm, Abdul Raḥmān and their likes. Then, following these names, come the names of the prophets and Imāms عليهم السلام; and the best of which is Muḥammad ﷺ. Nay, it is detestable to abandon this name if he had four sons; and it is detestable not to nickname the boy with Abā al-Qāssim if his name is Muḥammad.[77]

[77] Khumaynī, Sayyid Rūhullāh Mūsawī, *Taḥrīr al-Wasīlah*, Vol. 2, p. 281.

The Reasons for Virtuousness Within the Realm of Upbringing

The Seventh Day

The ʿAqīqah (The Sacrifice)

The aḥadīth of the infallible progeny ﷺ emphasized on the desirability of the ʿAqīqah on the seventh day after a child's birth. The ʿAqīqah is a sacrifice of a ram made on that day. In the Prophetic ḥadīth it is said, "When his seventh day comes, sacrifice a calf on his behalf."[78]

And the following ḥadīth points out the importance of the ʿAqīqah and its relation to the newborn child: "Every newborn is pawned to his ʿAqīqah."[79] This ḥadīth was interpreted to imply that the child is like a mortgaged thing which cannot be benefitted from until after its release. And since a child is a blessing; and a blessing is perfected upon its receiver once he is grateful for it, then gratefulness for this blessing is in the ʿAqīqah, as per the enactment of the Sunnah of the Messenger of God ﷺ.[80]

---

78 Al-Mīrzā al-Nūrī, *Mustadrak al-Wasāʾil*, Vol. 15, p. 140.

79 Al-Ḥurr al-ʿĀmilī, Shaykh Muḥammad b. al-Ḥasan, *Wasāʾil al-Shīʿa*, Vol. 15, p. 141.

80 Al-Tarihi, Fakhr al-Dīn, *Majmaʿ al-Bahrain wa Matlaʿ al-Nairain*, Vol. 15, p. 215.

The Prophet ﷺ implemented this Sunnah with al-Ḥasan and al-Ḥusayn (a). Asma' bint Omeiss narrated to us, as she was speaking of the birth of al-Ḥusayn (a), by saying, "... When his seventh day came up, the Prophet ﷺ approached me and said: Bring me my son, then he did with him as he did with al-Ḥasan (a); and he sacrificed a white ram on his behalf as he did on al-Hasan's behalf."[81]

The Etiquettes of the 'Aqīqah

Several etiquettes related to the 'Aqīqah were mentioned in the aḥadīth of Ahl al-Bayt (a); some of which are related to the child's future and virtuousness such as:

1. To sacrifice a male ram on behalf of the boy and a female ram on behalf of the girl.[82]

2. To feed the midwife part of the 'Aqīqah which is the leg with the hip.[83]

3. To feed from it ten Muslims, and the more the better.[84]

---

[81] Al-Ḥurr al-'Āmilī, Shaykh Muḥammad b. al-Ḥasan, *Wasā'il al-Shī'a*, Vol. 15, p. 142.

[82] Ibid., p. 148.

[83] Ibid., p. 152.

[84] Ibid.

4. The child's father and mother should not eat from the 'Aqīqah.

5. The 'Aqīqah should be fat; for in the ḥadīth it is mentioned: "The best of it is its fattest."[85]

6. To supplicate to God before sacrificing the 'Aqīqah by this supplication mentioned by Imām Ja'far al-Ṣādiq : "O people, I am innocent of what you are associating with God. I have directed my face to He who created the skies and earth like a true Muslim; and I am not of the polytheists. Indeed my prayer and my worship, my life and my death are for the sake of God, the Lord of all the worlds. O God, from You and back to You, in the name of God and God is the Greatest. O God, send your blessings to Muḥammad and the progeny of Muḥammad, and accept the deeds of X son of Y." And he mentions the newborn by his name, then he performs the sacrifice."[86]

---

[85] Al-Ḥurr al-'Āmilī, Shaykh Muḥammad b. al-Ḥasan, *Wasā'il al-Shī'a*, Vol. 15, p. 154.

[86] Ibid., p. 154-155.

7. To say when performing the sacrifice: "In the name of God, and by God, and Praise be to God, and God is the Greatest, believing in God and praising the Messenger of God ﷺ. Refraining from sin is upon His command, gratefulness is for His sustenance, and knowledge of His bounties belongs to us Ahl al-Bayt."

If he was a boy, he should say: "O God, you have bestowed upon us a male, and You are more knowledgeable of what You have bestowed; and it is from You that You have given. Accept whatever act we perform following the Sunnah of Your Prophet ﷺ. And ward off the cursed devil away from us. To You I have sacrificed blood, as You have no associate. And praise be to God, Lord of all the worlds."[87]

"O God, its meat with his, its blood with his, its bones with his, its hair with his, and its skin with his. O God, render it a protection for X son of Y."[88]

The ʿAqīqah of the Elderly

Highlighting the importance of the ʿAqīqah, the aḥadīth of Ahl al-Bayt ﷺ emphasized on the fact that it is desirable for a person whose parents didn't sacrifice a

---

[87] Ibid., p. 155.

[88] Ibid., p. 155-156.

ʿAqīqah on his behalf to sacrifice one for himself, even if he has become an elderly person. For, in the ḥadīth of Omar bin Yazīd, he said: I said to Abī Abdillah al-Ṣādiq : By God, I do not know whether my father had sacrificed a ʿAqīqah on my behalf or not; he said: Abu Abdillah commanded me and I sacrificed a "Aqīqah for myself while I was an elderly man.[89]

Shaving the Head and Giving Alms in Proportion to its Weight

One of the desirable acts of the seventh day after the child's birth is to shave his head and give alms in proportion to its weight by gold or silver.

In a ḥadīth by Imām Jaʿfar al-Ṣādiq , he said, "His head is to be shaved when he is seven days old; his hair is to be weighed with silver or gold and given as alms."[90]

Some narrations point out to the fact that it is required to dry out the hair from water before weighing it. For, it is narrated that Imām Jaʿfar al-Ṣādiq said, "One must sacrifice a ʿAqīqah on behalf of the newborn, pierce his ear, weigh his hair with silver after it is dried out, and

[89] Ibid., p. 145.

[90] Al-Ḥurr al-ʿĀmilī, Shaykh Muḥammad b. al-Ḥasan, *Wasā'il al-Shīʿa*, Vol. 15, p. 151.

give it away as alms. All this is to take place on the seventh day."[91]

Circumcising the Boy

It is well known that true Islam made it obligatory to circumcise the boy. This obligation remains all throughout his life as long as he hasn't fulfilled it. Narrations have emphasized on the desirability of performing the circumcision on the seventh day following his birth. For, it is mentioned that Amīr al-Mu'minīn, Imām 'Alī b. Abī Ṭālib said, "Circumcise your sons on the seventh day; do not allow the hot or cold weather to prevent you from doing so. For, it is a purity for the body; and the earth cries out to God from the defecation of the uncircumcised."[92]

It is narrated that the Prophet said, "Circumcise your sons on the seventh day; for, it is purer and quicker in growing skin." And he said, "The earth gets contaminated by the urine of an uncircumcised man for forty days."[93]

---

[91] Al-Mīrzā al-Nūrī, *Mustadrak al-Wasā'il*, Vol. 15, p. 145.

[92] Al-Ḥurr al-'Āmilī, Shaykh Muḥammad b. al-Ḥasan, *Wasā'il al-Shī'a*, Vol. 15, p. 153.

[93] Majlisī, 'Allamah Muḥammad Bāqir, *Biḥār al-Anwār*, Vol. 104, p. 124.

Moreover, it seems, from the narration that mentions a desirable supplication during circumcision, that circumcision has a moral impact on the future of the newborn boy.

For, it is narrated that Imām Ja'far al-Ṣādiq says, while circumcising a boy recite the followings: "O God, this is Your Sunnah and that of Your Prophet, may Your prayers be sent upon him and his progeny, and a manifestation of our compliance to You and Your religion according to Your Will and by Your Will to achieve something You have desired, a fate You have decreed and a matter You have fulfilled. Thus, you exposed him to the heat of iron during his circumcision and Hujama, for a reason which You are more aware of than me. O God, purify him from sins, prolong his life, keep all illnesses and pains away from his body, increase in his wealth and avert him from poverty. For, You know and we do not know."[94]

Up until this point, we have finalized the presentation of the factors that influence a child's virtuousness during the period preceding direct upbringing. As for the factors affecting his virtuousness through upbringing, they will be discussed below.

---

[94] Ibid., p. 124.

One of the certain desirable acts is sacrificing the ʿAqīqah for the male and female. It is also desirable for a male to perform the ʿAqīqah on behalf of the male and for the female to perform it on behalf of the female, and that it takes place on the seventh day. And if it gets delayed for a justified excuse or elsewise it doesn't lose its desirability. Rather, even though a ʿAqīqah was not performed on his behalf, he ought to perform it himself on his behalf. And even if he doesn't perform it during his life, it is desirable to have it performed on his behalf after his death. And it must be from one of the three following animals: 1- lamb, 2 – cow, 3- camel. And it is not fulfilled by giving alms with its price.[95]

It is desirable to shave the child's head on the seventh day and give silver or gold as alms according to the weight of the hair. It is detestable to shave a child's head from one side and leave it from another.[96]

It is mandatory to circumcise the males. It is desirable to carry it out on the seventh day, and it is acceptable to delay it. If it is delayed until after puberty, he must circumcise himself. Even in regards to the disbeliever, if

---

[95] Khumaynī, Sayyid Rūhullāh Mūsawī, *Taḥrīr al-Wasīlah*, Vol.2, p. 282.

[96] Ibid., p. 281.

he becomes a Muslim while he is uncircumcised, he must get circumcised even if he has become old in age.[97]

The Stages of Upbringing

We have spoken earlier of the factors that influence the creation of a virtuous child in the stage preceding the direct upbringing of the child. Here we will elaborate on what has been provided by the true Islamic *Sharīʿa* in regards to the upbringing of the child after it emphasized on its fulfillment in a proper manner and mandated that the person who carries it out properly receives God's ﷻ forgiveness. For, it is narrated that Imām Jaʿfar al-Ṣādiq ؑ said, "Honor your children and teach them good manners; and you will be forgiven."[98] And it was mentioned in a ḥadīth, "It is better for any of you to teach your child good manners than to give half a portion as alms every day."[99]

---

97 Ibid.

98 Al-Ḥurr al-ʿĀmilī, Shaykh Muḥammad b. al-Ḥasan, *Wasāʾil al-Shīʿa*, Vol. 15, p. 195.

99 Ibid.

The aḥadīth of the infallible progeny ﷺ elaborated, in detail, the stages of upbringing - according to the child's years of age. Thus, they have been divided into three which are:

1. The first seven years (1-7)

2. The second seven years (7-14)

3. The third seven years (14-21)

The Islamic narrations indicated the importance of providing the child with freedom during the first seven years, then disciplining, monitoring and chastising him for his actions during the second seven years, and then befriending him and making feel independent during the third seven years.

It is narrated that the Prophet of Islam ﷺ said, "A child is a master for seven years, a servant for seven years and a minister for seven years."[100]

Therefore, we will proceed in this book according to these three stages while starting off by the first seven years.

---

[100] Al-Ḥurr al-ʿĀmilī, Shaykh Muḥammad b. al-Ḥasan, *Wasāʾil al-Shīʿa*, Vol. 15, p. 194-195.

The First Seven Years (1-7)

During this age stage of the child's life, Islam emphasized on several matters which we will mention below:

1. Affection with Children

Ahl al-Bayt called for paying attention, during this sensitive stage of a child's life, to the emotional side which has a huge impact on his future.

For, emotional deficit and absence of care, love and tenderness towards the child may result in undesirable effects in his future. Moreover, some psychological studies point out to the fact that resorting to drugs might be rooted in parental emotional negligence which leads the child, in his teenage years, towards drug abuse.

Therefore, Islamic narrations emphasize on fulfilling the (child's) emotional needs. We realize this in Amīr al-Mu'minīn, Imām 'Alī b. Abī Ṭālib's , words to his son Imām al-Ḥasan , "I found you to be a part of me, nay I found you to be my entirety; to the extent that if something befalls you it is as though it has befallen me, and if death approaches you, it is as though it has approached me as well."[101]

2. Being Patient with Children

Islam commands parents to be patient with all that they encounter with their children, especially during the first seven years when the child acts in ways that exhaust his parents and worries them. For, he cries a lot, gets sick more often and plays mischievously. And based on the principle 'the child is a master for seven years', Islam orders (parents) to be patient with all this while pointing out the reward bestowed by God ﷻ upon parents or indicating the child's interest as he grows older.

We will present, below, a sample of aḥadīth that address the subject of patience with children.

Being Patient with Children's Crying

It is mentioned that the Prophet ﷺ said, "Do not beat your children when they cry; for, their crying is four months the testimony of 'there is no God but God', four months praying upon the Prophet ﷺ and his

---

[101] Majlisī, 'Allamah Muḥammad Bāqir, *Biḥār al-Anwār*, Vol. 74, p. 199.

progeny ﷺ, and four months supplication for his parents."[102]

Islamic history passed on to us the compassionate way in which the Prophet ﷺ used to deal with child's crying and screams. Once, when he was leading the noon prayer, he reduced and rushed the last two units of prayer (Rakʿahs). When he was done, people said: Did something happen during prayer? He ﷺ said, "What happened?" They said, "You rushed through the last two units of prayer (Rakʿahs). So, he ﷺ said to them, "Didn't you hear the boy's cries?" [103]

The Prophet rushed his prayer out of sympathy for the cries of the child whose mother left him to pray. He hurried in his prayer out of compassion for him.

Being Patient with Children's Illness

Just as Islam ordered parents to be patient with their children's crying, it ordered them likewise during their illness while pointing out the reward of doing so. For, it is mentioned that Amīr al-Muʾminīn, Imām ʿAlī b. Abī

---

[102] Al-Ḥurr al-ʿĀmilī, Shaykh Muḥammad b. al-Ḥasan, *Wasāʾil al-Shīʿa*, Vol. 15, p. 171.

[103] Ibid., p. 198.

Ṭālib said, in regards to the illness with which the child is inflicted, "an atonement for his parents."[104]

Playfulness with Children

In addition to the above, Islam emphasized on the necessity of having the parents understand the phase of childhood while dealing with children. For, the father – as well as the mother – must leave his position, social status and whatever his age demands in dealing with people to descend to the level of his child and play with him with kindness, tenderness and compassion. This has been indicated by the great Prophet in his saying, "He who has a child must behave childishly with him."[105]

It is also mentioned that Amīr al-Mu'minīn, Imām 'Alī b. Abī Ṭālib said, "He who has a child becomes like one."[106]

The Prophet practiced childishness with children, in front of the Muslims, when they saw him crawling while al-Ḥasan and al-Ḥusayn climbed on his back,

---

104 Ibid., p. 211.

105 Ibid., Vol. 15, p. 203.

106 Ibid.

and he ﷺ said, "The best of camels is yours, and the best of equals are you."[107]

These are some of the Islamic recommendations in regards to the positive treatment of children during this stage. Now, you will be presented with the recommendations regarding the negative treatment of children.

Prophets were sent by God ﷻ to nurture people and build the human being. And all prophetic books – especially the Noble Qur'ān – aim at bringing up the human being; for, through his upbringing the world will get reformed. And the harm caused by a person who hasn't been raised well by communities is incomparable to the harm caused by a devil, an animal or any other creature. And the benefits of a well-brought up person upon the communities is unmatched by any benefit received from a king or another beneficial creature.[108]

Wrong Behavior with Children

Some people think that the youthfulness of children allows them a great margin of unaccountability,

107 Majlisī, 'Allamah Muḥammad Bāqir, *Biḥār al-Anwār*, Vol. 42, p. 285.

108 *Manhajīyat al-Thawra al-Islāmīyah*, p. 224.

assuming that, in this stage, children do not get impacted by the way they are treated. However, it has been mentioned in religious texts that a child gets deeply impacted and is considered as a recipient during his first years. This influences the shaping of his character in the future; that's why Islam called for avoiding a set of things while dealing with children, some of which are:

1. Breaking Promises

Parents may make several promises to children then break them, assuming that this will not affect the shaping of the child's character due to his young age. However, the Noble Prophet ﷺ warned of the outcome of breaking promises made to children, due to the fact that a child looks at his parents as though they are the cause and source of his sustenance. And this perception has a great impact in a child's heart. Accordingly, if the parents break their promise, it will cause disappointment, in a child's heart, in the size of this perception. Moreover, a child views his parents as primary role models; thus, breaking their promise will cause lack of trust – from his side – in people's words after he lost trust in his primary role models. Therefore, it is mentioned that the noble Messenger ﷺ said, "Love children and be merciful with them. And if you promise them anything then keep your promise; for, they consider you the ones in charge of their sustenance."[109] And in another ḥadīth narrated on his behalf, he said, "If any of you makes a promise to his son, then he must fulfill it."[110]

It is narrated that Imām Abī al-Ḥasan said, "If you make a promise to children then fulfill it; for, they see that you are the ones providing them with their sustenance. God does not get angry for anything as much as he does for women and children."[111]

2. Inequality amongst Children

Some aḥadīth that are mentioned on behalf of Ahl al-Bayt warn from bias amongst children in regards to showing love and called for equality amongst children thereof. For, it is mentioned that the Messenger of God looked at a man who had two sons; the man kissed one son and left the other one. Thus the Prophet said, "Will you treat them equally?"[112]

Imām Jaʿfar al-Ṣādiq narrates on behalf of his father, Imām al-Bāqir, that he used to humor one of his

109 Al-Ḥurr al-ʿĀmilī, Shaykh Muḥammad b. al-Ḥasan, *Wasā'il al-Shīʿa*, Vol. 15, p. 201.

110 Al-Mīrzā al-Nūrī, *Mustadrak al-Wasā'il*, Vol. 15, p. 170.

111 Ibid., p. 202.

112 Majlisī, ʿAllamah Muḥammad Bāqir, *Biḥār al-Anwār*, Vol. 74, p. 84.

sons, put him on his thigh and break some sugar for him, even though righteousness belonged to another son. The Imām justified his behavior by saying, "They should not do to him as was done with Yusuf and his brothers. For, God did not send down a Sūrathexcept for compliance..."[113] This was an implication to the envy held by Yusuf's brothers against him due to the special care and obvious favoritism held by his father, Prophet Ya'qūb , towards him.

3.   Favoring Sons over Daughters

Islam rejected the favoritism of males over females on the basis of degrading the female and being pessimistic of her existence. For, it is mentioned that the Prophet said, "He who has a daughter, and does not get rid of her or insult her nor does he favor his son over her, God places him in Heaven."[114]

Moreover, in several aḥadīth, Islam considers daughters to be the best of children. One of them is mentioned by the Prophet , "The best of children are daughters - kind, organized, delightful, weeping and blessed."[115]

---

[113] Ibid., p. 78.

[114] Al-Mīrzā al-Nūrī, *Mustadrak al-Wasāʾil*, Vol. 15, p. 118.

[115] Ibid., p. 115.

In another ḥadīth said on his behalf ﷺ, "He who has one daughter has received that which is better than a thousand pilgrimages, a thousand conquest, a thousand camels and a thousand hospitalities."[116]

a. A Daughter is a Blessing

The Prophet of Islam ﷺ spoke of the angels' blessings called forth by the presence of girls in the house. For it is narrated that the Prophet ﷺ said, "There isn't any house that has girls within it except that, every day, twelve sorts of blessings and mercy descend to it from the sky, and the angels do not cease to visit that house and write for their father the reward of a year of worship for every day and night."[117]

b. Starting with the Girl

Islam asks the father to start with his daughter whenever he wants to distribute what he has brought to his children. For, it is mentioned that the Prophet of Islam ﷺ said, "He who enters the market, buys some goods then brings them to his children is like a person who has carried alms to a

---

[116] Ibid.

[117] Ibid., 116.

needy people. And he ought to start with the females before the males."[118]

c. The Girl First = Happiness

The Prophet ﷺ considered that one of the reasons for a woman's happiness is to have a daughter as her first child. For, it is mentioned on his behalf ﷺ, "It is a woman's happiness to have a daughter as her first child."[119]

d. Whoever Supports a Girl is with the Prophet

The Prophet ﷺ shows the honorable position of the person who supports a girl by saying – as was mentioned on his behalf, "He who supports one or two of the girls comes with me on the Day of Resurrection like these two", and he brought his fingers together.[120]

4. Having Sexual Intercourse in front of the Child

One of the things that Islam warns against is for the married couple to consummate their private

---

118 Ibid., p. 118.

119 Majlisī, ʿAllamah Muḥammad Bāqir, *Biḥār al-Anwār*, Vol. 104, p. 98.

120 Al-Mīrzā al-Nūrī, *Mustadrak al-Wasāʾil*, Vol. 15, p. 116.

relationship in a place that is accessible for the child to see and hear. For, this corrupts the child in his future and transfers him into a fornicator.

It is mentioned that Imām Ja'far al-Ṣādiq said:, "A man must not have intercourse with his wife or maiden while a child is in the house; for, this succeeds to fornication."[121]

It is also mentioned that the Great Prophet said, "By Him who holds my soul in His hand, if a man has intercourse with his wife while there is a child in the house who is awake, sees them and hears their words and breaths, then this child will never succeed. Whether it's a boy or a girl, the child will become a fornicator."[122]

An Invitation towards Shyness

Therefore, the true religion calls for shyness from others in regards to the private relationship. For it is mentioned that the Prophet 'Īsā said: "If any of you sits in his home, let him cover himself; for, God has decreed shyness as he decreed one's sustenance."[123]

---

121 Al-Ḥurr al-'Āmilī, Shaykh Muḥammad b. al-Ḥasan, *Wasā'il al-Shī'a*, Vol. 14, p. 94.

122 Ibid.

123 Ibid., p. 96.

One of the interesting and wise sayings is what is mentioned by Imām Jaʿfar al-Ṣādiq ☙, "Learn from the crow three attributes: concealing himself with copulation, his earliness in seeking out his sustenance and his cautiousness."[124]

"O women, it is from your laps that the ascending must take place. In your laps, the children must be raised according to the proper Islamic upbringing. For, the child grows up in your laps, adheres to you, and his eyes and ears are attracted towards you. If he hears his mother lie, he may become a liar. Whereas, if he sees his mother to be a balanced person and his father a virtuous person, then he will become a virtuous man."[125]

The Second Seven Years (7-14)

Based on the division of the age stages of a child that was made by the honorable Prophet ☙ which mentioned that 'a child is a master for seven years, a servant for seven years and a minister for seven years'[126], we will continue the discussion on the second stage which is the stage of discipline.

---

[124] Ibid., p. 94.

[125] *Al-Marʾa fī Fikr Āyatullāh Sayyid Khumaynī*, p. 157.

[126] Al-Ḥurr al-ʿĀmilī, Shaykh Muḥammad b. al-Ḥasan, *Wasāʾil al-Shīʿa*, Vol. 15, p.195.

1. Teaching Children
2. The Influential Human Factors in Upbringing
3. Hitting Children

It starts with teaching children.

Teaching Children

Islam has given great importance to teaching children; and the Prophet of Islam ﷺ spoke of the reward of that action by saying, "If the teacher says to the child: 'In the name of God', God grants him, the child and his parents exoneration from Hellfire."[127]

It is also mentioned on his behalf ﷺ, "It is better for a man to discipline his child than to give half a portion as alms every day."[128]

---

127 Al-Mīrzā al-Nūrī, *Mustadrak al-Wasā'il*, Vol. 15, p. 116.

128 Ibid.

The narrations of the Infallibles guided towards teaching children through the following:

1. Teaching Writing

The Prophet considered that it is the child's right upon his father to teach him writing. This has been manifested in his well-known ḥadīth, "A child has three rights upon his father, to give him a good name, to teach him how to write and to marry him once he reaches puberty."[129]

It seems, from some narrations, that the sixth year of a child's age is appropriate for teaching him writing. For, it is mentioned that Imām Ja'far al-Ṣādiq said, "Hold your son until he reaches the age of six, then discipline him through writing at the age of six..."[130]

2. Teaching the Qur'ān

The aḥadīth of the Ahl al-Bayt urged parents to teach their children the Noble Qur'ān. It indicated the abundant reward to be given to the parents who contributed to his learning of God's majestic book. It is mentioned that Amīr al-Mu'minīn, Imām 'Alī b. Abī Ṭālib said, "He who kisses his child gains a reward;

---

[129] Ibid.

[130] Majlisī, 'Allamah Muḥammad Bāqir, *Biḥār al-Anwār*, Vol. 104, p. 95.

and he who makes him happy, God makes him happy on the Day of Resurrection. And the parents who teach him the Qurʾān get summoned and dressed up with garments whose radiance lights up the faces of the people of Heaven."

The narrations of the Infallibles   guided towards teaching the girl Sūrat al-Nūr due to the great meanings enclosed therein in regards to the topic of women in Islam. Meanwhile, the narrations prohibited teaching her Sūrat Yūsuf, perhaps so that her mind does not grow around the atmosphere of the perverted women's society from which the Prophet Yusuf   suffered. For, it is mentioned in a ḥadīth that the Prophet   said, "One of the child's rights upon his father is... if she was a female... to teach her Sūrat al-Nūr and refrain from teaching her Sūrat Yūsuf."131

3. Teaching the Right Theologies

The Imāms of Ahl al-Bayt   ordered fathers to take the initiative and teach their children the true Islamic theology, that is, before they start hearing some misleading fallacies that may have an impact on themselves once they do not know the answers to it especially in societies where theological fallacies and

---

131 Al-Ḥurr al-ʿĀmilī, Shaykh Muḥammad b. al-Ḥasan, *Wasāʾil al-Shīʿa*, Vol. 15, p. 100.

perverted ideas are raised against the sphere of righteousness. Therefore, it is necessary to guard children before they confront that society; and in this context it is mentioned that Amīr al-Mu'minīn, Imām 'Alī b. Abī Ṭālib said, "Teach your children of our knowledge that which God makes useful to them, so that the Murjites do not conquer them with their opinions."[132]

It is also mentioned that Imām Ja'far al-Ṣādiq said, "Take initiative with sharing the aḥadīth with your children before the Murjites beat you to it."[133]

4. Teaching the Legal Rulings

In addition to guarding the child theologically, parents must teach him the rulings of what's permissible (*ḥalāl*) and what's forbidden (*ḥarām*) so he can start abiding by them, especially during the period that precedes his puberty and age of duty. For, it is necessary for the father to teach his son the signs of puberty through which he becomes dutiful of abiding by God's rulings, and the rulings through which he is tried during his lifetime. The same applies to the mother who should teach her daughter the true Islamic rulings. Thus, the

---

132 Ibid., p. 197.

133 Ibid., p. 196.

child will welcome his puberty with clarity, steadiness, consciousness and maturity.

Unfortunately, we find that teaching the child the rulings of what's permissible and forbidden is lacking in many of our Islamic communities. For, it has been observed that people focus on teaching their children only the knowledges of the worldly life; and they may even prohibit them – in certain cases – from learning the rulings of Islam. This was foreseen by the Messenger of God when he said, "Woe to the children of the end of times from their parents." Someone asked him: O Messenger of God, from their polytheistic parents? He said, "From their faithful parents who do not teach them any of their obligations. And if their children aspire to learn them they prohibit them from doing so. And they get pleased with them for trivial matters of this worldly life. Thus, I absolve myself from them and they absolve themselves from me."[134]

5. Teaching Prayer

Ahl al-Bayt emphasized on teaching prayer to children. In some narrations, it has been mentioned that the child is ordered to pray at the age of nine, and is held accountable for it once he reaches the age of duty.

---

134 Al-Mīrzā al-Nūrī, *Mustadrak al-Wasā'il*, Vol. 15, p. 164.

It is narrated that Amīr al-Mu'minīn, Imām ʿAlī b. Abī Ṭālib said, "Teach your children prayer, and make it obligatory for them once they reach the age of duty."[135]

It is also narrated that Imām Jaʿfar al-Ṣādiq said,: "The child regains his teeth[136] at the age of seven and is ordered to pray at the age of nine."[137]

In some narrations, the command to pray starts from the age of seven; for, it is narrated that Imām Mūsā al-Kāẓim said, on behalf of his fathers, that the Messenger of God said, "Command your children to pray when they reach the age of seven..."[138]

6. Commanding Children to Join Both Prayers

In pursuit of mitigating the burden on children so they don't feel the heaviness of prayer upon them, Imām Jaʿfar al-Ṣādiq called for commanding children to join the prayers of Ẓuhr and ʿAṣr, and the prayers of Maghrib and Ishā'. For, on one hand, joining them is permissible; and on another hand, it eases the process

---

[135] Ibid., p. 169.

[136] The child is taught prayer once he regains his teeth, i.e. after his teeth grow back after his baby teeth have fallen.

[137] Al-Ḥurr al-ʿĀmilī, Shaykh Muḥammad b. al-Ḥasan, *Wasā'il al-Shīʿa*, Vol. 15, p. 183.

[138] Al-Mīrzā al-Nūrī, *Mustadrak al-Wasā'il*, Vol. 15, p. 16.

for them. It is narrated that Imām Jaʿfar al-Ṣādiq said, "We command our children to join between the Ẓuhr and ʿAṣr prayers, and between the Maghrib and Ishā' prayers as long as their ablution is still effective and before they get busy with other affairs."[139]

This was the practice of Imām Zayn al-ʿĀbidīn as well who, according to the narrations, used to command the children to pray the Ẓuhr and ʿAṣr prayers at the same time, and the Maghrib and Ishā' prayers at the same time. He was asked about this, so he said, "It is less burdensome upon them and it is better for them to rush for it and not miss it, nor sleep on it or get distracted from it." And he only ordered them with the mandatory prayer[140] (i.e. he did not order them with the desirable prayer.)

7. Teaching the Poetry of Abī Talib

Amīr al-Mu'minīn, Imām ʿAlī b. Abī Ṭālib – as per the narrations – was fond of having the poetry of his father, Abī Ṭālib, recited and written down. And he used to say, "Learn it and teach it to your children; for,

---

139 Al-Ḥurr al-ʿĀmilī, Shaykh Muḥammad b. al-Ḥasan, *Wasā'il al-Shīʿa*, Vol. 15, p. 183.

140 Al-Mīrzā al-Nūrī, *Mustadrak al-Wasā'il*, Vol. 15, p. 160.

it is in line with the religion of God and it encloses a lot of knowledge."[141]

We will mention, here, some of Abī Ṭālib's poetry which he said to his nephew, the Prophet Muḥammad ﷺ:

You invited me and I knew you were honest And you were honest and, beforehand, you were trustworthy.

And I knew that the religion of Muḥammad is the best of all mankind's religions.[142]

8. Teaching Swimming and Archery

In addition to its emphasis on teaching the above, Islam stressed on teaching children swimming and martial arts, so that the child becomes capable of defending himself and protecting the true religion of God. This was mentioned on behalf of the Prophet ﷺ, "Teach your children swimming and archery."[143]

---

[141] Ibid., p. 166.

[142] Al-Amin, Muhsin, *A'yān al-Shī'a*, Vol. 1, p. 324.

[143] Al-Ḥurr al-'Āmilī, Shaykh Muḥammad b. al-Ḥasan, *Wasā'il al-Shī'a*, Vol. 15, p. 194.

The noblest work in the world is raising a child and providing society with a real human being.[144]

You must pay attention to the fact that the school phase is more important than the university phase. This is because the intellectual perfection of the adolescent is carried out during the former phase.[145]

Within the knowledge that starts in the name of the Creator, lies the light of guidance.[146]

The Human Factors of Upbringing

Despite the impact of teaching on molding children's personalities and their behavioral performance, nonetheless, the human environment surrounding the child may play an even bigger role than teaching. One can speak of the role of this environment under the following titles:

1. Parents

It is observed that, in addition to being influenced genetically by his father and mother as was previously

[144] *Al-Kalimāt al-Qiṣār*, p. 247.

[145] Ibid., p. 247.

[146] Ibid., p. 249.

mentioned, the child's character gets highly influenced by the parents' behavior. For, if the child learns lying from his parents, he may never abstain from lying as long as the role models in his life lie. The same applies to other attributes.

Therefore, the aḥadīth of Ahl al-Bayt warned about the parents' responsibility for their behavior and its impact on the child. For example, these aḥadīth commanded parents to be honest in their interaction with their child; as it was mentioned in the Prophet's speech that he said to parents, "... And if you made them a promise then fulfill it."[147]

The child may also get influenced by his parents by ways other than upbringing. For, when the child sees his parents in constant quarrel, it will be reflected negatively on his personality. However, if he gets used to them being in a state of amiability and agreement, he will learn from them to love others. And perhaps this is what Amīr al-Mu'minīn, Imām 'Alī b. Abī Ṭālib points out in his saying, "The amicability between parents brings forth closeness amongst the children."

---

[147] Al-Ḥurr al-'Āmilī, Shaykh Muḥammad b. al-Ḥasan, *Wasā'il al-Shī'a*, Vol. 15, p. 201.

2. The Teacher

The impact of the teacher on building the child's character is quite visible, especially if we observe how the child perceives his teacher which more often resembles the way a follower perceives his role model. For, it has been concluded in some statistics conducted in one of the countries that 35% of children desire to become like their teachers and follow their path. It was rather said that the fall of Andalusia was due to the upbringing of children at the hands of Christians.

The nation's late Imām, the great Khumaynī, used to focus a lot on the role of teachers and their influence on their students. He used to say, "All sorts of happiness and misery rise from schools. And the key, thereof, lies in the teachers' hands."[148] Therefore, parents must be very careful to the quality of schools in which their children are enrolled and to the quality of teachers thereof, due to their huge impact on their personalities.

3. Colleagues/Mates

This indicates the child's friends whether they were schoolmates or neighbors or otherwise. For a child

[148] Khumaynī, Sayyid Rūhullāh Mūsawī, *al-Kalimāt al-Qisār*, publications of the institute of Tanzim wa Nashr Turath al-Imām al-Khumaynī, Tehran, p. 274.

frequently picks up his mates' habits and morals. Accordingly, it is the child's right upon his father to place him in a good environment, as was mentioned in the story of the man who came to the Prophet ﷺ and said to him, "What is my child's right? "He ﷺ answered, "To give him a good name, teach him good morals and place him in a good environment."[149]

There are many cases that contribute, to a large extent, in a child being influenced by his friends:

The First Case: It's the case where the family is separated which could take place due to the death of the father or mother, or divorce or constant quarreling between the parents. For, when a child moves outside the house, in pursuit of escaping the state of psychological turmoil he is suffering from, he will sense his need for friends which increases his susceptibility to being influenced by them.

The Second Case: When the family moves to a new environment, such as when a family moves to a new city or another neighborhood. Then, the child will look for new friends and sense his need for their friendship, which will lead him towards being influenced by them.

---

[149] Al-Ḥurr al-ʿĀmilī, Shaykh Muḥammad b. al-Ḥasan, *Wasāʾil al-Shīʿa*, Vol. 15, p. 198.

Therefore, parents – in such cases – must be highly attentive to the child's new relationships.

The Third Case: The stage of puberty and adolescence. For, in this stage, the child develops the desire for being independent from his parents, which pushes him towards strengthening his relationship with his friends.

4. Prominent Individuals

The child looks, in admiration, at prominent individuals in society such as community leaders, country leaders, religious scholars or athletes or artists, which develops – in him – the ambition to become like one of them.

Herein comes the role of the parents to embed, within their children's hearts, the love, attachment and devotion to divine leaders. Thus, they should teach them the biography of the Prophets and Imāms, and implant their love within their hearts.

Also in this category, God and the Prophet direct their focus towards the love of Ahl al-Bayt so they can become role models for the Islamic community, and so that the hearts of generations get attached to them out of love for them and in pursuit of being close to them.

Therefrom, it has been determined who we should love:

The first beloved is Muḥammad ﷺ on whose behalf his saying was mentioned, "A person is not considered a believer unless I am dearer to him than his son, father and all people."[150]

After his love comes the love of Ahl al-Bayt (a) which God ﷻ has made the reward for the message of Islam when He ﷻ said:

﴿قُل لَا أَسْأَلُكُمْ عَلَيْهِ أَجْرًا إِلَّا الْمَوَدَّةَ فِي الْقُرْبَىٰ﴾

﴿qul lā 'as'alukum 'alayhi 'ajran 'illā l-mawaddata fī l-qurbā﴾

﴿Say, 'I do not ask you any reward for it except the love of [my] relatives.'﴾[151]

Then, a group of people came to the Prophet ﷺ and said, "O Messenger of God, who are your relatives

---

[150] Rayshahrī, Āyatullāh Muḥammad, *Mīzān al-Ḥikmah*, publications of al-Dār al-Islāmīyah, Beirut, Vol. 2, p. 237.

[151] Sūrat al-Shūrā, Verse 23.

whose love was mandated?" He ﷺ said, "Alī, Fāṭima and her two sons."[152]

A teacher is a trustee. However, the object of this trusteeship is different from all other deposits. For, he has been entrusted with a human being.[153]

Let the main concern engulfing teachers be their own self-refinement, so that their words can influence others.[154]

Hitting Children

Hitting is of Two Kinds

Islam rejected hitting as a primary and chief means to raising children. However, it did not reject it entirely. It rather accepted it as the last available means to resolve the issue of child corruption under special conditions which reduce its magnitude and directs it towards the path of healthy upbringing. Accordingly, under Islam, hitting is of two types: rejected and accepted.

---

[152] Ṭabāṭabā'ī, 'Allamah Sayyid Muḥammad Ḥusayn, *Al-Mīzān fī Tafsīr al-Qur'ān*, publications of Dār al-'Alami, Beirut, Vol. 18, p. 52, al-Razi, al-Tafsīr al-Kabir, publications of al-'I'lam al-Islami, 3rd edition, p. 166.

[153] *Al-Kalimāt al-Qisār*, p. 274.

[154] Ibid., p. 274.

The Reasons behind the Rejected Hitting

Hitting a child stems, frequently, from a state of anger which the father or mother experiences due to a behavior conducted by the child. This appears in the general scenery. However, if we delve deeper into it, we will discover several reasons behind hitting children such as:

1. Sense of Possessiveness

Parents, frequently, feel like they have a right of ownership towards the child. Therefore, each of them believes that he can do whatever he wishes with him. This feeling acts as an unconscious reason behind hitting the child.

2. The Child's Weakness

Parents feel that their child is weak; thus, they may take advantage of this point to exercise their authority and control over him. And this harshness, on the parents' side, may be a reaction to an authoritarian approach being exercised against them.

For example, the father may be oppressive against his wife whereby he hurts her by hitting her and so, then, the wife (mother) releases the severe anger she holds against her husband onto her weak child.

3. Ignorance of the Phase of Childhood

Harshness against children and hitting them may rise from parents' ignorance of the childhood phase and its experiences. For example, the child may carry out some childish behaviors that can be unbearable for his father who isn't aware of the fact that it's very natural for someone his age to do these things; thus, he reacts and hits the poor child.

4. Being Inconsiderate of the Change of Times

Practicing violence against children may also rise from the lack of awareness of the change in times that affects the social environment according to which the child behaves, when the parents do not understand the change that has occurred.

Islam's Confrontation against the Reasons of Rejected Hitting

We find that the Islamic teachings provided satisfying responses to the reasons behind hitting mentioned above:

First: Islam did not grant parents the right of ownership towards their children. Islam didn't even give man the right of self-ownership; for, according to the Islamic law, it is impermissible for someone to use even his body as he wishes. For, he cannot inflict upon himself certain types of torture, how then would he be entitled to own others?!!

Second: Islam called for treating children's weakness with sympathy and mercy. For, it is narrated that the Prophet ﷺ said, "Love children and have mercy on them."[155] And on behalf of Amīr al-Mu'minīn, Imām ʿAlī b. Abī Ṭālib ؑ, it is narrated, "Let their elderly half mercy on their youth."[156]

Third: Islam guided parents towards the necessity of understanding the phase of childhood, and to the fact that the father – for example -, regardless of his status and position, must descend to the level of the child in his relationship with him. This was mentioned on behalf of the Prophet of Islam ﷺ in his saying, He who has a child should behave childishly with him."[157]

Fourth: Islam asked parents to be understanding of the change in time and circumstances that surround society which calls for a reflection on forcing the child or prohibiting him from certain things – as long as it still

---

[155] Al-Ḥurr al-ʿĀmilī, Shaykh Muḥammad b. al-Ḥasan, *Wasā'il al-Shīʿa*, Vol. 15, p. 201.

[156] Bayḍūn, Labīb, *Tasnīf Nahj al-Balāgha*, p. 745.

[157] Al-Ḥurr al-ʿĀmilī, Shaykh Muḥammad b. al-Ḥasan, *Wasā'il al-Shīʿa*, Vol. 15, p. 203.

falls under the permissible acts according to the *Sharīʿa*. This is what Amīr al-Muʾminīn, Imām ʿAlī b. Abī Ṭālib pointed out when he said:,"Do not force[158] your children onto your manners; for, they are born in a different time than yours."[159]

Acceptable Hitting and its Conditions

Islam didn't approve of hitting to be the primary means of resolving an issue with the child; rather, the father or mother must resort to a lighter means before resorting to it.

This would be to make him feel a sort of emotional deficit. For, the mother or father who manages to fill the child's heart with affection and tenderness can rely on the impact of this affection when he shows his frustration with the child's behavior and abandon him for a short period of time, so that the child can tremble at the core of his emotions and refrain from repeating this behavior. This means was mentioned by Imām Abī al-Ḥasan when someone complained to him about

---

[158] To force someone against their desire.

[159] Majlisī, ʿAllamah Muḥammad Bāqir, *Biḥār al-Anwār*, Vol. 104, p. 99.

his son. He ✿ said, "Do not hit him; rather abandon him... but not for long."[160]

And the Imām's ✿ warning in regards to refraining from long abandonment serves to protect the child from becoming harsh and cold-hearted.

If this emotional cure does not work, along with guiding the child through conversation, then the means of hitting emerges as the last and exclusive resolution.

However, the requirements of acceptable hitting should be taken into consideration in order to maintain its effectiveness in influencing the child. Otherwise, the opposite would take place.

The Conditions of Influential Hitting

The First Condition: Hitting must be in pursuit of disciplining the child, and not due to a psychological state of anxiety where the child serves as a punching bag for stress release.

The Second Condition: The child must understand that the hitting and punishment are due to his improper behavior which he has committed. Parents should aim at having the child fear his own sin and the Lord who is watching over him, rather than his father or

---

[160] Al-Falsafi, *al-Tufl bayn al-Wiratha wal-Tarbiya*, p. 393.

mother. For, if the fear is targeted towards the father or mother, then the child will repeat the wrong doing in their absence. Whereas if he is raised upon fearing his own wrongdoing and the fact that God watches him as he commits it, then this will keep him from committing this horrible action even when his parents are absent. Moreover, the fear of one's own wrongdoing and the feeling of divine monitoring preserve – in the child – the attributes of courage and fearlessness from others.

Amīr al-Mu'minīn, Imām 'Alī b. Abī Ṭālib pointed out this educational remark when he said, "One must not have hope except in God, and must not fear except his own sin."[161]

The Prophet also pointed out to the aforementioned – that fear must not be from the parents – in his saying, "Woe to him who is obeyed out of fear from his oppression, woe to him who is honored out of fear from his wickedness."[162]

The Third Condition: He must not exaggerate while hitting the child; he must rather be gentle with him. For, the aim is to draw his attention to the vileness of his action so he can refrain from it. And this does not align

161 Ibid., p. 389.

162 Ibid., p. 384.

with severe hostility; it rather takes place through gentle hitting. Imām Jaʿfar al-Ṣādiq ❀ called attention to this issue when he was asked about disciplining the child, so he said, "five or six, and be gentle."[163]

In another narration, it is mentioned that someone told Imām Jaʿfar al-Ṣādiq ❀, I may have hit the boy for a misconduct he committed.

He ❀ said: How many times did you hit him?

The man said: Perhaps a hundred times.

He ❀ said, "A hundred? A hundred?!!" He repeated it twice, then he said: "This is the penalty for fornication, fear God!"

The man said: How many times should I hit him?

He ❀ answered: Once.

The man said: By God, if he knew that I would hit him only once he wouldn't have left anything without corrupting it.

He ❀ said: Then twice.

---

163 Khūʾī, Āyatullāh Sayyid Abū al-Qāsim Mūsawī, *Mabānī Takmilat al-Minhāj al-Ṣāliḥīn*, publications of Dār al-Zahra', Beirut, Vol. 1, p. 340.

The man said: This is my doom! He kept contesting until he reached five times. Then he ﷺ got angry and said: "O Isḥāq, if you know the penalty for his misconduct then implement it and do not trespass the limits of God."[164]

The Taxes for Hitting

As an emphasis on refraining from hurting a child through excessive hitting, Islam imposed a fiscal tax on the parent who harshly hits the child and leaves a trace on his body.

We will present, below, the rulings related to mandatory taxes imposed due to hitting a child.

[164] Ibid., p. 340-341.

a. On hitting the face and changing its color without any wounds, breaks, swelling or disease, we present the following table:

Change in facial color due to the hitting	The Tax in Dinars	The Tax in Gold
When the face reddens.	One Dinar and a half	5.4 grams
When the face becomes green.	3 Dinars	10.8 grams
When the face becomes black.	6 Dinars	21.6 grams

b. On hitting the body and only changing its color, we present the following table:

Change in the body due to the hitting	The Tax in Dinars	The Tax in Gold
When the body reddens.	0.75 Dinars	2.7 grams
When the body becomes green.	1.5 Dinars	5.4 grams
When the body becomes black.	3 Dinars	10.8 grams

c. On wounding the head and face, we present the following table:

The Type of Wound on the Head and Face	The Tax
If the skin is peeled without bleeding.	A camel
If the wound slightly enters the skin which allows for blood to come out.	Two camels
If the wound severely enters the skin and does not reach the thin skin which covers the bones.	Three camels
If the wound severely enters the skin and pierces through the thin skin which covers the bones.	Four camels

The Third Seven Years (14-21)

Proceeding with the noble prophetic division of a child's age 'a child is a master for seven years, a servant for seven years and a minister for seven years'[165], we will continue our discussion on the third stage which is the stage of befriending the child and cooperating with him.

165 Al-Ḥurr al-ʿĀmilī, Shaykh Muḥammad b. al-Ḥasan, *Wasāʾil al-Shīʿa*, Vol. 15, p. 195.

A Double-edged Sword

This stage of man's life is considered to be extremely sensitive in both positive and negative connotations. For, it is either invested to become the most important opportunity from which man can benefit, or it can lead its owner to the valleys of vice and corruption. We have examples for both situations.

Regarding the case of positive investment, we find it in the young men of the Islamic Resistance in Lebanon who brought back dignity to the Islamic nation in their war with the Zionist enemy. Many of them are of this age.

And we find the decline into vice in the following report on the youth in America: "Suicidal incidents have increased with the youth ranging between the age of 15 and 34; and the number of suicidal incidents in the United States reached 28,500 last year."[166]

Ahl al-Bayt emphasized that this stage would be a double-edged sword. It can either be invested in obedience or it will lead man towards disobedience. For, here, we find Amīr al-Mu'minīn, Imām 'Alī b. Abī Ṭālib telling his son al-Ḥasan in his will, "... The heart of

---

[166] Al-Zaʿbalāwī, *Tarbiyat al-Murāhiq*, publications of the institute of al-Kutub al-Thaqafiyya, Riyad, 1414 AH, p. 434 copied from al-Ahram newspaper.

a child is like empty land; it accepts whatever is placed within it. Thus, I took the initiative and taught you discipline before your heart hardens and your core gets distracted..."[167]

The Occurring Changes during this Stage

During this stage, a person encounters two types of changes, one in his body and another in his psychological state.

Bodily Changes

As for the body:

a. The throat widens and the vocal cords grow twice as long in males which causes the depth of voice.

b. The bones and body increase in height.

c. A person's weight increases around 16 kilograms (about 35 pounds) within two years (14-16 in girls and 16-18 in males.)

d. Hair appears in various body parts.

---

167 Sharīf Raḍī, Muḥammad b. al-Ḥusayn, *Nahj al-Balāgha*, Sermon/Letter/Saying 31.

e. The sexual instinct emerges.[168]

Sexual Awareness-Raising

One of the most important risks during this stage is that which is related to the sexual instinct of the youth at this stage.

Herein emerges the parents' role in raising their children's awareness on this sensitive issue.

Puberty

It is crucial for the father or whomever the father delegates to introduce the child to the issue of puberty, whereby he introduces him to two things:

First: that puberty transfers the person to the realm of religious accountability in front of God ﷻ. For, once it occurs, the pen of penalty starts writing on a board which he will see published on the Day of Resurrection.

Second: how puberty takes place, and that it has three signs for males.

1. Reaching 15 lunar years (about 14 years and 6 months in solar years).

---

168 Al-Qā'imī, *Osos al-Tarbiya*, publications of Dār al-Nubala', Beirut, p. 252-253.

2. The growth of thick hair on the pubic area (which is the area below the end of the stomach).

3. The emergence of sperms through wet dreams or otherwise.

Thus, the boy will not be surprised when he wakes up to find himself with ejaculated semen; rather, he gets introduced to the new stage of his life wherein monitoring is indispensable.

Illegitimate Sex

One of the things that are required from the father in pursuit of raising his son's awareness is to introduce him to the impermissible sexual acts and their risks, in order to refrain from them. Thus, he introduces him to the dangers of fornication and its disadvantages in this worldly life and the Hereafter. And it is desirable to share with him the *Sharīʿa*-based aḥadīth on fornication, such as the ḥadīth of the great Prophet ﷺ, "Fornication comprises six attributes, three of them are in this worldly life and the other three in the Hereafter:

For the ones in the worldly life:

1. It eliminates one's glory.

2. It rushes one's death.

3. It suspends sustenance.

As for the ones in the Hereafter:

1. Severity of one's penalty.
2. The anger of God, the Compassionate.
3. Dwelling in the Hellfire."[169]

It is also desirable to share with him the verses that were mentioned in regards to fornication, especially those which indicate the penalty of a fornicator, such as His ﷻ saying:

﴿الزَّانِيَةُ وَالزَّانِي فَاجْلِدُوا كُلَّ وَاحِدٍ مِنْهُمَا مِائَةَ جَلْدَةٍ ۖ وَلَا تَأْخُذْكُمْ
بِهِمَا رَأْفَةٌ فِي دِينِ اللَّهِ إِنْ كُنْتُمْ تُؤْمِنُونَ بِاللَّهِ وَالْيَوْمِ الْآخِرِ ۖ
وَلْيَشْهَدْ عَذَابَهُمَا طَائِفَةٌ مِنَ الْمُؤْمِنِينَ﴾

﴿az-zāniyatu wa-z-zānī fa-jlidū kulla wāḥidin minhumā mi'ata jaldatin wa-lā ta'khudhkum bihimā ra'fatun fī dīni llāhi 'in kuntum tu'minūna bi-llāhi wa-l-yawmi l-'ākhiri wa-l-yashhad 'adhābahumā ṭā'ifatun mina l-mu'minīn[a]﴾

---

[169] Rayshahrī, Āyatullāh Muḥammad, *Mīzān al-Ḥikmah*, publications of al-Dār al-Islāmīyah, Vol. 4, p. 240.

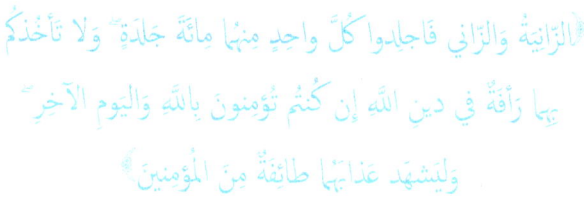

﴾As for the fornicatress and the fornicator, strike each of them a hundred lashes, and let not pity for them overcome you in God's law, if you believe in God and the Last Day, and let their punishment be witnessed by a group of the faithful﴿.[170]

Furthermore, it is one of the father's missions to introduce his son to the impermissibility of masturbation, its risks and what God ﷻ prepares for its committer in the worldly life and the Hereafter. For, God ﷻ considers it one of the great forbidden acts.[171]

He must also introduce his son to the dangers of abnormal sexuality; for, it is mentioned that it shakes the throne of God ﷻ.[172]

The Path of the Forbidden Sexual Acts

It is not sufficient for the father to warn his son about the risks of the forbidden sexual acts and their impermissibility; he must rather warn him about the risks of the paths that lead towards these acts. We will present below some of these paths.

---

[170] Sūrat al-Nūr, Verse 2.

[171] Khū'ī, Āyatullāh Sayyid Abū al-Qāsim Mūsawī, *Mabānī Takmilat al-Minhāj al-Ṣāliḥīn*, Vol. 1, p. 346.

[172] Shīrāzī, Āyatullāh ʿAbdul Ḥusayn Dastaghīb, *al-Dhunūb al-Kabīrah*, translated by al-Qabanji, publications of al-Dār al-Islāmīyah, Vol. 1, p. 11.

1. Being Deceived by Beauty

A young man may get deceived by his own handsomeness which may lead him towards forbidden sex. Thus, narrations drew attention to this issue; as it was mentioned in a ḥadīth: "On the Day of Resurrection, the man who was deceived by his beauty in the worldly life will be called forth, and then he will say: O Lord, you gifted me beauty by which I was deceived. Then, Yūsuf is called forth, and the man is asked: Who is more beautiful? You or him? We have gifted him beauty, yet he was not deceived."

On the other hand, it is narrated that the Prophet said, "The most loved creature to God is a young man who has a beautiful image and who dedicated his youth and beauty for the sake of God and in the way of obeying Him. This is the person who (God) the Gracious flaunts in front of his angels and says: 'this is my true servant."

2. The Forbidden Gaze

Looking at women with a lustful gaze is one of the paths that may lead towards forbidden sex. Thus, God commanded people to lower their gaze. And it is mentioned in the aḥadīth of Ahl al-Bayt that looking at that which God has forbidden is considered as fornication of the eye.

﴿قُل لِّلْمُؤْمِنِينَ يَغُضُّوا مِنْ أَبْصَارِهِمْ وَيَحْفَظُوا
فُرُوجَهُمْ ۚ ذَٰلِكَ أَزْكَىٰ لَهُمْ ۗ إِنَّ اللَّهَ خَبِيرٌ بِمَا يَصْنَعُونَ﴾

﴿*qul li-l-mu'minīna yaghuḍḍū min 'abṣārihim wa-yaḥfaẓū furūjahum dhālika 'azkā lahum 'inna llāha khabīrun bi-mā yaṣnaʿūn*a﴾

﴿وَقُل لِّلْمُؤْمِنَاتِ يَغْضُضْنَ مِنْ أَبْصَارِهِنَّ
وَيَحْفَظْنَ فُرُوجَهُنَّ وَلَا يُبْدِينَ زِينَتَهُنَّ إِلَّا مَا ظَهَرَ مِنْهَا﴾

﴿*wa-qul li-l-mu'mināti yaghḍuḍna min 'abṣārihinna wa-yaḥfaẓna furūjahunna wa-lā yubdīna zīnatahunna 'illā mā ẓahara minhā*﴾

﴿Tell *the faithful men to cast down their looks and to guard their private parts. That is more decent for them. God is indeed well aware of what they do. And* tell *the faithful women to cast down their looks and to guard their private parts, and not to display their charms, except for what is outward...*﴾[173]

And it is mentioned that he ﷺ said, "There isn't anyone who hasn't committed one aspect of fornication. For,

[173] Sūrat al-Nūr, Verse 30-31.

the fornication of the eye is the gaze, and that of the mouth is the kiss, and that of the hand is the touch."[174]

3. Friends

It is noticed that teenagers discuss sexual matters and love affairs to a large extent, which may have an influence of the individual's sexual behavior. Therefrom emerges the parents' role to monitor the quality of their child's friends and aim to surround him with virtuous friends and companions.

The Prophet ﷺ warned – as was mentioned on his behalf – about the impact of the friend and companion in a gentle way by saying, "The example of a virtuous companion and a bad companion is like a holder of musk and a blower in a bellow."[175]

For, a holder of musk either transfers his musk to his companion such that the latter becomes perfumed as well, or at least allows the latter to smell from him the musky scent. Whereas in the case of the person who blows in the bellow[176], its fire may reach the person and

[174] Shīrāzī, Āyatullāh ʿAbdul Ḥusayn Dastaghīb, *al-Dhunūb al-Kabīrah*, Vol. 1, p. 211.

[175] Al-Zaʿbalāwī, *Tarbiyat al-Murāhiq*, p. 421.

[176] A bellow is a device with an air bag that emits a stream of air when squeezed together with two handles, used for blowing air into a fire.

burn him, or – in case that doesn't happen – the latter will sense from it a bad smell.

The Solution

In pursuit of resolving the sexual issue for a young man, Islam suggests early marriage which it considers to be one of the child's rights upon his father.

For, it is mentioned that the Prophet ﷺ said, "A child has three rights upon his father: to give him a good name, to teach him writing and to marry him once he reaches puberty."[177]

Some educational schools[178] confirmed this Islamic theory when it realized that the real solution to this problem is early marriage which will stand in the way of a huge battle between the young man and the devil. Accordingly, it was mentioned that the Prophet ﷺ said, "No man gets married in his young age except that his devil wails: Woe to him! Woe to him! Woe to him! He has protected two thirds of his religion from me."

The desirability of early marriage includes, both, males and females. For it was mentioned that, "Maidens are

---

177 Majlisī, 'Allamah Muḥammad Bāqir, *Biḥār al-Anwār*, Vol. 104, p. 92.

178 Al-Qā'imī, *Osos al-Tarbiya*, p. 258.

like fruit on trees, if it matures without being reaped, the sun will damage it and the wind will scatter it away. Likewise, when maidens realize womanhood the only remedy they have is to get married."[179]

It is also mentioned that Imām Jaʿfar al-Ṣādiq ﷺ said, "One of man's joys is not to have his daughter embark on menstruation in his house."[180]

Psychological Changes

With the start of these years (14-21), some psychological needs appear in an adolescent which he tries hard to fulfill. We will present some of these needs below.

1. The Need for Independence

With the rise of his teenage years and undergoing the physical changes, the teenager develops a tendency towards the love of independence from his father and mother. He may even take a path of rebellion against them after having lived the previous years submissive to their will.

---

[179] Khumaynī, Sayyid Rūhullāh Mūsawī, *Taḥrīr al-Wasīlah*, Vol. 2, p. 220.

[180] Ibid.

The teenager feels that stepping out of his parents' authority allows him to fulfill his manhood and that he is not a child anymore.

Islam came, in this sensitive stage, to address the child from one side and the parents from another.

In regards to addressing the parents, Islam asks them to change the way they treat their child; for, the stage of being a 'servant' has ended and the stage of being a 'minister' emerged. He is, now, a 'minister for seven years.'

Ministry implies giving the child a sort of independence; however, it doesn't mean giving him absolute independence. What is intended from this expression is for the parents to introduce the child to society, its conditions and problems, so he can benefit from their experiences and knowledge and have his path towards independence enlightened through them.

As for addressing the child, Islam asks the child to maintain a positive attitude towards his parents which does not get disturbed by huffing in their face, nor by giving them a gaze of resentment. Otherwise, God will not accept any of his prayers.

2. The Need for Appreciation

A teenager, after reaching puberty, feels a need to have a social status through which society appreciates him.

Islam wants to have this need fulfilled through the proper divine path and a sincere intention directed towards God.

And the Islamic rulings and history are witnesses to the provision of youthful adolescents with a social status. For, the Messenger of God ﷺ assigned Usāma b. Zayd as the leader of the Islamic army despite his young age whereby people objected and said, "He put the senior Immigrants and Companions under the command of a boy."[181]

It was also said that he was fifteen years old.[182]

Moreover, we have read in the history of Karbalā' names of young adolescents from Banū Hāshim who marked the greatest heroic epic while they were in this age such

---

[181] Ibn Hishām, *Sīrat al-Nabī* ﷺ, verified by ʿAbd Hamīd, publications of Dār al-Fikr, Beirut, Vol. 4, p. 328.

[182] Al-Zaʿbalāwī, *Tarbīyat al-Murāhiq*, p. 411.

as Ja'far b. 'Alī b. Abī Ṭālib who was nineteen years old at the moment of his martyrdom.[183]

Worship and Education

Parents must address the teenager's need for appreciation in the proper manner, in order for him to be concerned, mainly and primarily, with God's perception of him.

This takes places through education which was encouraged by Islam, especially during the age of adolescence. For, it is mentioned that Imām Mūsā al-Kāẓim said, "If I find a Shī'a adolescent who does not learn jurisprudence I will strike him with my sword."[184]

Knowledge is that which leads him towards true servanthood to God, so that he becomes an example of the ḥadīth mentioned on behalf of the Prophet of Islam, "Seven people are in the shade of God's throne on the day when there is no shade except His: a just ruler and a young adolescent who was nurtured upon the worship of God."[185]

---

183 Shams al-Dīn, Muḥammad Mahdī, *Ansar al-Ḥusayn*, publications of al-Dār al-Islāmīyah.

184 Rayshahrī, Āyatullāh Muḥammad, *Mīzān al-Ḥikmah*, Vol. 5, p. 8.

185 Ibid., p. 9.

May God support the fathers and mothers with the upbringing of their children, so that they become virtuous children in the worldly life and Heaven's flowers in the Hereafter. Praise be to God, the Lord of all worlds.

www.ingramcontent.com/pod-product-compliance
Lightning Source LLC
Chambersburg PA
CBHW051002140626
46546CB00017B/2419